JEROME SAVONAROLA

HIERONYMI·FERRARIENSIS·A·DEO
·MISSI·PROPHETE·EFFIGIES·

Portrait of Savonarola by Fra Bartolomeo della Porta (circa 1498).

JEROME SAVONAROLA
A Sketch

JAMES L. O'NEIL, O.P.
Edited and revised by Jules Samuels

STUDIO FRATESCO

MMXXIV

Originally published in 1898 by Marlier, Callanan & Co. (Boston).
Published by Arouca Press in cooperation with
Studio Fratesco and The Savonarola Society.

ISBN: 978-1-998492-08-4 (pbk)
ISBN: 978-1-998492-09-1 (hc)

Arouca Press   The Savonarola Society
PO Box 55003   A daughter organisation
Bridgeport PO   of the OP Prayer apostolate.
Waterloo, ON N2J 0A5   336 Impasse de la Brousse,
Canada   Salignac-Eyvigues,
www.aroucapress.com   Dordogne,
Send inquiries to   France, 24590
info@aroucapress.com

Book and cover design by
Alexander Norton, Studio Fratesco

NOS INFRASCRIPTI Revisores Ord. Praed. pro scriptis excudendis fidem facimus quod attente perlectum opusculum cujus titulus "Jerome Savonarola," a Rev. Fr. J. L. O'Neil, O. P., compilatum, typis mandari posse censemus. In quorum Fidem his propria manu subscripsimus. Datum in Collegio nostro Sti. Joseph Ohiensi, apud Somerset, die 16 Junii, 1898.

FR. JOSEPH KENNEDY, O.P., STUD. REGENS.
FR. AUGUSTINUS WALDRON, O.P., S.T.L.

IMPRIMATUR:

FR. LAURENTIUS FRANCISCUS KEARNEY, O.P.,
Prior provincialis

Bostoniae, Julii 25, 1898.

IMPRIMATUR:

GULIELMUS BYRNE, V.G.
in Diocesi Bostoniae
Ordinarius Agens

Contents

PART II

APPENDICES

THE SAVONAROLA PROJECT

The republication of Fr. O'Neil's two works on Savonarola is among the first efforts of a significantly larger project dedicated to the comprehensive study of the Friar's life, preaching, writings, and doctrine through the first-ever English translation of his *opera omnia*, which consists of over 25 volumes. This translation project will provide unprecedented access to his sermons, writings, and letters, with the aim of not only clarifying and rehabilitating his historical reputation but also offering a reliable guide and pastor, conformed to the heart of Christ, to souls who desire to live virtously and advance in the spiritual life. The project also encompasses the translation and publication of important works concerning the Friar, such as the biographies written by Fra Pacifico Burlamacchi and Giovanfrancesco Pico della Mirandola, and studies, such as Paolo Luotto's *Il Vero Savonarola e il Savonarola di L. Pastor.*

Critics have long exploited the narrative of a corrupt Church during Savonarola's time, with both Protestants and Revolutionaries attempting to claim him as their own. The statue of Martin Luther in Worms, which positions Savonarola at Luther's feet as a supposed precursor, is just one example of this misrepresentation. However, we will demonstrate that Savonarola was not a forerunner of revolutionary ideologies but rather a champion of true Catholic reform. He stands as a testament to the enduring sanctity of the Roman Catholic Church, even during her darkest times. As astonishing as it may seem, his life and teachings serve as a direct censure and refutation of the errors that would later fuel the Protestant revolt. To more accurately reflect the truth of history, the statue at Worms would better depict Savonarola stepping on the mouth of Luther, silencing his blasphemies and dismantling his falsehoods.

There is a pressing need for Savonarola's historical rehabilitation, and, if deemed worthy by the Sovereign Pontiff, canonical glorification. Savonarola's unwavering commitment to truth, often mischaracterized as fanaticism or delusion, was none other than a consistent application of the faith according to a Christian conscience properly formed in the school of the Angelic Doctor, St. Thomas Aquinas, and in the contemplative silence of the cells of San Domenico in Bologna and San Marco in Florence.

This project is critical to the initial stages of gathering documentation for the potential canonisation of Savonarola which was requested by the Dominican Order in 1935 and continues slowly today. By making these primary sources accessible in English for the first time, we seek to inspire contemporary readers with Savonarola's preaching, doctrine, asceticism, prophecies, contemplation, mysticism, reforms, and martyrdom. His was an exemplary life of virtue, sanctity, fidelity to the Roman Catholic Church and the Sovereign Pontiff, and love for Our Lord Jesus Christ. Five centuries later, Father Girolamo's life and word still have the power to reinvigorate the spiritual and moral fibre of individuals and of society at large.

There are a number of seemingly insurmountable difficulties with a project like this. Translation costs alone make similar projects financially unviable for large publishers, who either underpay translators or avoid the publication altogether. We are fully aware of these challenges and, after receiving wise counsel from experienced academics and scholars, have opted for a hybrid model to help crowd-fund this project. The structure is simple but unique, and relies on the support of generous patrons to cover translation, design, and publication costs.

For more information on the project and its developments, or to support the project financially, visit: patreon.com/savonarola or x.com/savonarolasoc.

SCHEME OF WORKS

Sermons

Philosophy and Theology

Spiritual Works

PREFACE

✠

THIS LITTLE VOLUME is issued in commemoration of
the fourth centenary of the death of Jerome Savonarola, who was executed on May 23rd, 1498. I have
not approached the subject with any notion of presenting the
famous preacher in a new light, nor have I written for scholars
to whom the copious literature on Savonarola is available, but
for those to whom many of these works may not be accessible.
In the first part of this sketch, the public career of Savonarola is
presented after the manner of a chronicle; in the second part,
I have endeavoured to give a picture of the man, illustrated by
his own writings, which are considered in an appendix. For the
convenience of those of my readers who may desire to pursue
the subject in a more comprehensive way, I add a second appendix, containing a list of books that will be found of service. I
have drawn from some of these works, and have consulted, at
first hand, all the contemporary sources, but I do not consider
it necessary to encumber the pages of this volume with detailed
references. A general credit and acknowledgment must suffice,
particularly as my obligations to a majority of the authors named
is slight, while I am much indebted to other sources of value

which are not specially mentioned. Passion, in most loyal devotion and in most malignant enmity, centred around the friar during life. Time has not silenced the voice of hate or of love. If the Italian laureate, Carducci, in his blasphemous "Hymn to Satan," hails Savonarola as one through whom Lucifer wrought havoc amongst mitres and crowns, saints have regarded him as a martyr and saint.[1] In applying the terms "martyr" and "saintly" to Savonarola, I am mindful of the decree of Urban the Eighth, to which I profess entire submission. The saying attributed to the great Pope Benedict the Fourteenth, who venerated the friar, —"If God gives me the grace to win Heaven, as soon as I shall have consoled myself with the Beatific Vision, my curiosity will lead me to look for Savonarola," —vividly expresses a thought awakened in many minds during the last four hundred years. The alleged declaration of Pius the Seventh, that in Heaven we shall know why the Jesuits were suppressed, and the meaning of Savonarola's death, is probably the last word of criticism for all practical purposes.

Feast of St. Catherine of Siena,
April 30, 1898

---

1 Years have probably conferred greater discretion on Carducci. Recently he made a public declaration that the celebration of Savonarola's fourth centenary was not appropriate for him or his kind; that only devout and intelligent Catholics should participate in it.

PART I

I

ANCESTRY AND EARLY DAYS OF SAVONAROLA

✠

O N THE 21ST of September, in the year 1452, was born the most illustrious citizen of the ancient Italian city of Ferrara, Jerome Savonarola.[1] The family of Savonarola was of Paduan extraction. Jerome's grandfather, Michael, was a celebrated physician in Padua, where for two hundred years his ancestors had won distinction and esteem. The fame of Doctor Savonarola induced Nicholas the Third, Lord of Ferrara, to urge his coming to that city. He accepted the invitation, and as physician to the prince took up his residence at the court. Of his son Nicholas, the father of Jerome, nothing notable is recorded. A shiftless man, a physician without ambition, but an acceptable follower of the court, he failed to share the renown attaching to the name of Michael, who was justly distinguished for his medical writings as well as for his skill in practice. Jerome was one of seven children. Of his earliest years, we have few particulars. Neither playful nor pretty, he was a grave child, studious, and

---

1 Ferrara, now a poor town of scarcely thirty thousand people, was then a city of one hundred thousand inhabitants, and as the capital of the House of Este, the scene of much splendour, a home of Italian culture and pagan learning, the stately host of visiting princes, emperors, and popes, to whom royal welcome was magnificently extended.

devoted to his mother. These are the characteristics that most deeply impressed themselves on observers and biographers, and they sum up the exterior child life of this remarkable man.[2] As he entered upon his growing boyhood, the seriousness of the child deepened. He soon recognized the vanity and pomp of a society which was largely pagan in its refinement. He conceived such an abhorrence for it that, having once been brought to the duke's palace, he resolutely declared that he would never again visit the place. Study and prayer filled his days, while meditation made more firm his increasing conviction that the times were evil. His parents intended him for the medical profession, but Divine Providence had otherwise ordained. In the learning of his day, Savonarola made rapid progress; for as Burlamacchi, afterwards his religious brother and disciple, tells us, he worked night and day. The philosophy of Aristotle and of Plato he diligently read, following these by an ardent and enthusiastic study of the Angelic Doctor.

---

2   The period which witnessed the birth and childhood of Savonarola marks the close of the Middle Ages, ushers in the Renaissance, and is at once the dawn of a new spiritual life for the Church, and a harbinger of the dread Reformation. He was a nursing infant when Constantinople fell, and the last of the Greek emperors, (blessed) Constantine XI Paleologus, gave way to the conquering Turk, Mahomet the Second; when Scanderbeg was fighting, and St. John Capistrano, the famous Franciscan, was preaching for the cause of Christian Europe. The fifteenth century was not only an era of religious and political activity, but of general restlessness, of social turbulence, of mercantile enterprise, of maritime expeditions, of impulsive ambitions. The invention of the art of printing from movable types; the improvement in methods of manufacturing paper, with the consequent cheapening and multiplying of books; the introduction to "Western Europe, through a multitude of scholarly (Grecian refugees, of the riches of Oriental culture, not only in their native Greek, but in the store of Arabic, Chaldaic, and Syriac literature, henceforth to form a part of the intellectual life of the West; and of a fuller classical learning, the renewal of studies which had never perished, especially in monastic schools,— were among the causes that, in the seething womb of this peculiar epoch, struggled for the birth of a new life. During the period when these various forces were in a condition of fermentation, the minds of many were anxious and harassed, and spiritual men foresaw and proclaimed that some great, because necessary, change must come in the affairs of Church and state. As the century advanced in its second half, the immortal discoverer Christopher Columbus, whose voyages were to open a new world for the Church and civilization, was dreaming his divine dreams, and looking out over the unknown seas with eyes of yearning and with a heart eager for exploration, and inspired by zeal for the salvation of souls. These two famous Italians did not meet in this world; but in starry regions of peace and bliss, we trust that their much-tried spirits have found rest and recompense with God.

While he thus enriched his mind, devotion and piety alone in his manner and conduct, the fruit of the growing charity with which his tender heart glowed. Fidelity to his books prepared him for that wider and deeper research which came later, in reading the lessons of the human heart. Full of sympathy as he witnessed squalor, suffering, and ignorance side by side with luxury, indulgence, and pagan culture, his soul burned with righteous indignation against the irreligious and unchristian spirit which was dominant, and with tender pity for God's neglected poor. As the gulf, already broad, grew wider and wider, "the rich becoming richer and the poor poorer," his spirit cried out in the crude but impassioned verses which he entitled "On the Ruin of the World." To him the whole world seemed awry, virtue and piety having disappeared, sin walking abroad without shame, bloodshed and rapine triumphant, the widow and the orphan despoiled, Christ scorned, and Heaven defied. Savonarola was then only in his twentieth year. We may easily credit Father Marchese when he tells us that at this time the youth found pleasure in the woods, in lonely places, walking in the fields or by the river's bank, singing plaintively or weeping, thus giving vent to the emotions which surged in his breast. For an account of an interesting incident of this period of his life, we are indebted to Father Benedict, one of his disciples at San Marco's, who learned from the master many details of his youth.

Living near the Savonarola homestead in Ferrara was a Florentine exile of the noble house of the Strozzi, whose daughter attracted the attention of the gloomy young poet. A sudden attachment sprang from this, doubtless a passing emotion of fancy, under the influence of which Savonarola declared to the lady his devotion. We may judge the just indignation with which he met her haughty rejection, her cutting announcement that no Strozzi could stoop to an alliance with a Savonarola. This shattering of his hopes, this disappearance, as he then thought, of all light and sunshine, was the happy occasion of his turning more completely to God. The piety which he had always cultivated now urged him to an absolute abandonment of the world. He did not act hastily; but considered the matter long, seeking guidance through prayer. When he was about twenty-two years old, as he mentions in one of his discourses, and as Pico della Mirandola, Burlamacchi, and Father Benedict also record, he heard a sermon delivered by an Augustinian friar. So deep an impression did this preacher make on him that his resolution was at once formed to leave the world and to join a religious order. His love and admiration for St. Thomas Aquinas determined his choice of the Order of Preachers. Nevertheless, another year passed before he effected his purpose. During this time his tender heart suffered unspeakable anguish, for the delay was entirely due to his fear of inflicting pain on his father and mother by announcing to them his purpose of retiring to a monastery.

II

The Cloister—Ideal of the Religious Life (1475-1481)

✠

THE STRUGGLE WAS ended only in 1475. On April
24th, being then in his twenty-third year, Savonarola
stealthily left his home and set out for Bologna and St.
Dominic's, where the sacred relics of the Patriarch lie enshrined
in the noble and exquisite tomb wrought by Niccolo Pisano, the
cradle of modern Christian art.[1] Savonarola's earliest ideal was
the religious life in its simplest form, the work and lowliness of
a lay brother seeming to him the more attractive. This erroneous notion was dissipated by the Fathers of St. Dominic's, who
pointed out to the student that the career to which he was called
was that of the priesthood.

---

1 For the consolation of his father and mother he wrote a letter and a brief tract
on contempt of the world. These they found after his departure. The letter is deeply
religious. Declaring the feelings of love and reverence for his parents which were
deep in his heart, he gently reminds them that he could not have trusted himself
to bid them adieu. In a subsequent letter he tells them that he is about to become
a soldier of Jesus Christ, an honour which they will assuredly prize above the
fleeting honours of this world's wars and heroes. In his tract he emphasised these
sentiments, expressing at the same time, in vigorous language, his horror of the
sinful world which he is about to abandon. He begins, even in this youthful pro-
duction, to announce the coming wrath of God in punishment of Italy's sins.

In the retreat at Bologna, Savonarola spent seven happy years. Prayer, fasting, mortifications of the most rigorous kind, filled his days; at the same time, his modesty and obedience proved how truly he had separated himself from the outer world. During this period he lectured to the novices, composed a Compendium of Philosophy, and wrote commentaries on Plato, his previous philosophical and theological studies having laid a most solid foundation for the vast learning which he subsequently acquired.

Early in his religious life his meditations, which before his coming to Bologna had found expression in the canticle or poem, already mentioned, on the ruin of the world, bore further fruit in a second metrical composition, which he styled *The Ruin of the Church*. Brooding over the unhappy condition of his beloved Italy (for Savonarola was no mere provincial), witnessing a period whose annals deal frequently with treachery, cruelty, bloodshed in war, in riot, and in assassination, his gloomy forebodings were further embittered as he beheld the relaxation in morals, the scandals in ecclesiastical life, the decay of faith, the numerous disorders which afflicted the Church. In this canticle on the sins prevailing among the faithful, his ardent soul pictures with a sombre vividness the evils that had already come, and the misfortunes that, as a necessary consequence and punishment, would follow in their train, he describes the Church in solitude, mourning the overthrow of her chaste edifice, spending her days in tears because of the havoc that had been wrought. His inflamed imagination beheld the evil spirit as a horrible vampire that had spread its great wings over the prostrate form of the Church, from which it gradually drew the lifeblood. Then, as if rapt in an ecstasy of indignation, the impetuous young friar poured out the longings of his soul "for the beauty of the house of the Lord," and for the honour of the place where His glory dwelleth: "O God, O Lady, give me that I may break those spreading wings! that I may slay this monster Church! that I may lift up and restore your beloved Church."[2] His gracious Lady bade him be silent, to pray and weep. With a swelling heart, he obeyed, giving himself to the life of the cloister in the fullest devotion of his generous soul. Thus, restrained by the Spirit of God, and yielding to the empire of grace, he rigorously devoted himself to the vocation with which he had been honoured.

2 We have paraphrased the impassioned words of the young friar. These verses supply the key to his future career.

III

ARRIVAL IN FLORENCE
(1482)

✠

HISTORY IS SILENT as to the time of Savonarola's first appearance in the pulpit. Even the date of his ordination is not given by his biographers. Certain it is, however, that while in Bologna his superiors directed him to preach. What effect these discourses had on his audience we know not. Apparently, he did not achieve any notable success, for contemporary chronicles make no mention of his efforts. In 1481 he was sent to Ferrara, his native city, where for a time he preached, but without any special influence. Apart from a lack of polish that many of the cultured hearers of those days considered more important than doctrine, his want of success may have been an illustration of the old proverb, that a prophet is not without honour, save his own country. So, at least, Savonarola thought.

During this year, the closing of the University of Ferrara, the faculty of which included several members of the Dominican Order, was the occasion for the withdrawal of some of the brethren previously assigned to the convent of that city. Savonarola was sent to the Tuscan capital, destined afterwards to be the scene of his triumphs and his sorrows. He never again saw his native place. The contemplation of the misfortunes which threatened Ferrara and all Italy through expected war, stirred the soul of the anxious friar as he began his journey to his new home. We know not whether the gloom of his reflections was brightened by the beautiful panorama which opened up before him in the very heart of the garden land of Italy, as he gazed, for the first time, on the lovely valley in which fair Florence, divided by the River Arno, sat gloriously enthroned, and solemnly guarded by the lordly Apennines. Nor may we judge whether, as he entered the noble convent of San Marco, a prophetic inspiration fell upon his soul, or coming events cast their shadows on the hopes that must have swelled his generous heart while he thought of this new and extensive field which awaited his labour and zeal. The name of San Marco's is forever linked with the history of Florence, with the career of Savonarola, and with the memory of the Medici; for it was Cosimo the Elder who built and endowed the convent at a heavy cost, and there welcomed the Dominicans in the year 1443. To this great man, the brethren were further indebted for a magnificent library, which was practically the first public library founded in Italy.

The friars of San Marco's were men of learning as well as of piety; and under their fostering care, especially in the golden days of St. Antoninus and of Bl. Fra Angelico, San Marco's became the centre of Christian culture in Florence. Only twenty-two years had elapsed since the death of the gentle archbishop when Savonarola entered the convent whose walls were all alive with the speaking figures of Angelico's lovely saints and angels, and with the glory of Paradise itself, and whose chronicles were enriched with the story of his brother Dominican artists. Learning and art and sanctity, therefore, greeted the young friar from Ferrara and bade him welcome to this home of religion and true Christian erudition. Beyond its peaceful cloister, there arose

the din and strife of politics and of contending philosophers.[1]
Not only were purely religious studies neglected,[2] but even the
pursuit of full and genuine profane learning was neither serious
nor dignified.

Lorenzo the Magnificent discussed Plato with his followers
[3]and then passed to the composition of obscene carnival ballads and rhymes whose merits his sycophantic courtiers lauded
beyond the immortal song of Dante. Such was the standard
among the men who venerated everything ancient, who regarded
"the discovery of a Greek or Latin manuscript as one of the greatest blessings of Heaven," who extravagantly extolled the classics,
and endeavoured, through a blind imitation of Greek and Latin
writers, to establish a neopagan literature. So lamentable a measure of life, among the higher classes, accompanied as it was by
much immorality, induced a corresponding degradation of the
people. Vice, it may be said, was too often unchecked, unrebuked. The Carnival was not a mere diversion preceding Lent;
it was a prolonged dissipation in which lewd displays and ribald
songs, some of the latter composed by Lorenzo, were a large part
of the programme. The contamination of public manners was a

1   While in other parts of Europe politics, as we now understand the term, was an
unknown factor, in Italy a number of petty states, variously named, including one
kingdom, several duchies, republics, and marquisates, had so fostered the spirit
of diplomacy and statecraft, that in the fifteenth century the science of politics
had made rapid advance in popular interest and study. Florence probably deserved
the primacy of eminence in the tangled and crooked work which this study and
interest developed among the turbulent and often fiercely contentious Tuscans.
Among the *literati* of this time, the amenities of literary life were often observed
by charge and countercharge of fraud, treachery, crime, etc., "the flowers with
which the glorious path of scholarship was strewn."

2   At this time, as Savonarola declared in one of his sermons, there was not a
professor of Holy Scripture in all Florence, outside of the monasteries, and even
in them he claimed that the sacred study did not flourish.

3   The Academy of Plato, which had been founded by Cosimo de' Medici, was then
under the presidency of the famous Marsilio Ficino. Its members often engaged
in debate on theological and philosophical questions, having in view the reconciliation of Christianity with paganism! Of Ficino himself it is recorded that the
Gospels were Platonised before he could relish them. While thus marking with
a note of severity those scholars who were puffed up with pagan lore, we are not
unmindful of those who, like Pico della Mirandola, that marvel of genius and
learning, had preserved their faith, and even later cultivated devotion.

necessary consequence of these entertainments. Hallam, speaking of Lorenzo the Magnificent, whose patriotism he could not praise as disinterested, declares that he completed the subversion of the Florentine republic for which his two immediate ancestors had prepared, the mockery and pageant of forms having alone been preserved by him in order to keep up the illusion of liberty. A student of Tacitus, Lorenzo realised that, in imitation of the Roman Emperor Augustus, the most effective way to carry out his purpose of enslaving the people was first to corrupt them. Nor had he read the life of Pericles without learning the same lesson from the Athenian tyrant. It is not, therefore, surprising that the political condition was deplorable among a people whose republican institutions had previously and successfully resisted oft-repeated shocks, but who now seemed, with few exceptions, dead to all thought of freedom. Verily, the proud Catholic Republic had sunk low when Savonarola began his labours among the Florentines.

IV

Beginning of Savonarola's Career
as a Preacher and Missionary
(1482-1489)

✠

I T REQUIRED BUT a short time for Savonarola to appreciate
his new surroundings. Occupied with the instruction of the
novices, he had, however, no opportunity of appearing in
the pulpit till the Lent of 1482. These few months of preparation
were providential. They enabled him to study the difficulties of
his position and served as a judicious check on what might have
been a rash precipitancy had he spoken in the first fervour of
his indignation. Seeing how the Bible was held in slight esteem,
having been superseded by Plato and Aristotle among many of
the learned, he gave himself with renewed determination to
the study of the Scriptures, inculcating at the same time a like
devotion on the part of his novices. The Divine Word was indeed
his armoury. During all the succeeding years of his preaching,

he invariably made the Holy Scriptures the root and basis of his discourses.[1]

Disregarding the prevailing method of address, and speaking from his big, honest heart, without quibble or subterfuge, seeking neither to please cultivated ears nor to win pagan applause, he began his Lenten sermons in the church of San Lorenzo. His earnestness, his fire, his wealth of Scripture learning and comment, were all lost on the Florentines who came to hear him. Their sense of pagan art and refinement was shocked by the bluntness of the man who cared more for truth than for its forms. As Lent drew to its close his audience had dwindled to twenty-five, women and children included. Assuredly a discouraging beginning for the ardent champion of faith and virtue in this demoralised centre of infidelity and immorality! Nevertheless, he accepted the lesson, while he recognized the cause of his failure; and though his soul flamed with the message he felt that God wished him to deliver, he resolved to retire, and resume in the quiet of San Marco's his commentaries on the Bible which he then knew by heart. These lectures were primarily intended for his beloved "angels," as he called the white-robed boys of San Marco's, who had come to follow in the way of him whom Dante named—

> "The loving minion of the Christian Faith,
> The hallowed wrestler, gentle to his own,
> And to his enemies terrible."

Subsequently, however, as we shall see, others sought admittance and were kindly received. In the Lent of 1484, and again in 1485, Savonarola was sent as preacher to the little republic of San Gimignano, among whose people simplicity went hand in hand with faith and piety. Strangers to the refinements and the debaucheries of Florence, they listened with reverence and

---

1   "He delighted," Father Marchese tells us, "in the Bible as a perennial fountain of inspiration. Like Dante, Michelangelo, Milton, he drew from the sacred pages beauties which entitle him to rank with the immortals." Possibly Savonarola's great love of the Bible may have been seized as a pretext by those who, unlike him, rejected the authority of the Church as a divinely appointed interpreter, to class him with Protestants.

in a truly penitential spirit, as the orator gave free vent to his righteous indignation because of the prevailing sins of Italy. At San Gimignano, he foretold some of the calamities which subsequently fell upon the land.[2] During the succeeding four years Savonarola varied his scholastic work by preaching in various towns. In the summer of 1489, his superiors withdrew him from the missionary field and recalled him to San Marco's.[3]

At first, he discoursed only to the brethren, but soon his fame spread; and despite that Lombard tongue which grated on Tuscan ears, laymen crowded to hear the man whose power they felt, and to whose words they listened as the utterance of one who knew whereof he spoke. San Marco's could not contain all who wished to share in the lecturer's teaching. Despite his unsparing labours, these were days of rest, of calm, of preparation for the greater labours and for the trials that were in waiting. "Thus," as Mrs. Oliphant gracefully writes, "the first chapter of Fra Girolamo's history ends, under the damask rose tree in the warm July weather, within those white cloisters of San Marco. In the full eye of day, in the pulpit and the public places of Florence, as prophet, spiritual ruler, and apostle among men, was the next period of his life to be passed. Here his probation ends."

2   In 1484 he also preached in Brescia, to the people of which he declared that certain defined chastisements would fall on them. The fulfilment of this prediction Madden and other biographers find in the scourge of 1500, which came with the pillage of the town by the French. Assuredly, the coincidence is striking.

3   For the statement of Villari and others that this change was made at the request of Lorenzo de' Medici there is not sufficient evidence. A seeming basis for their supposition they find in an incident that occurred in 1482. In that year Savonarola attended a Chapter of his Province held at Reggio. Among the distinguished scholars who were present as guests of the Brethren, interested in the disputations which relieved the more solemn and formal features of such assemblies, was Pico della Mirandola. Either because of a personal introduction to Savonarola as the opening of an acquaintance, or merely through admiration aroused by his talents, Pico formed a strong attachment to the friar. A few years later, it is alleged, he used his influence with Lorenzo to secure the permanent assignment of Savonarola to San Marco's. That the Dominican Superior should accede to such a request, if made by Lorenzo, would not have been inconsistent with religious discipline, especially as the growing reputation of the young lecturer had already become the theme of frequent discussion among the Florentines. If Lorenzo did procure the recall of Savonarola, he probably had no anticipation of the consequences involved, nor did he think that in this friar he would find his firmest opponent on behalf of Florentine liberty and reformation.

Portrait of Lorenzo de' Medici from the workshop of Bronzino (circa 1565).

V

LENTEN DISCOURSES—PRIOR OF SAN MARCO—
RELATIONS WITH LORENZO DE' MEDICI
(1490-1492)

✠

YIELDING TO THE urgent requests of the laymen who
thronged the spacious cloisters and garden to hear his
discourses, Savonarola announced, towards the end of
the month, that on Sunday, Aug. 1st, 1490, he would speak from
San Marco's pulpit; and, as Burlamacchi tells us, he added, "I
shall speak for eight years." He delivered his first discourse, feeling that he had indeed entered on a divinely appointed work.
This he outlined in three propositions, the spirit of which pervaded his sermons during the entire period of his public ministry. The Church of God, he declared, needs reformation;[1] Italy
will be scourged; and these things will soon come to pass. With
these propositions as texts, and with the wealth of Scripture as a
storehouse from which to draw, he scattered with a lavish hand
the gathered fruits of years spent in meditation, in prayer, and
in grief for the unhappy conditions prevailing. "Swift and fiery"
was the natural eloquence of the man, who, arguing that mere

---

1   From within, and only in discipline and morals.

elegance of diction was of minor importance, disregarded many of the forms prescribed by art.

The effect produced on the Florentines by the friar's sermons was notable. Some held him to be a man of God, a prophet; others claimed that he was a fanatic, to whose raving denunciations sensible men would pay no heed. That his opponents, as well as admirers; continued to flock to San Marco's, overtaxing the capacity of the convent church, proves the extraordinary interest awakened and sustained by the preacher who vigorously censured the vices of his time, and confidently foretold the coming calamities, chastisements sent by the God of justice.

That great "contradictions" arose against him, as Burlamacchi declares, we may readily believe. It could not have been otherwise. He had anticipated this; he knew that prophets had been for himself he foretold the same fate. The friar's study of his Divine Master had been too loving and faithful to leave any doubt in his mind, or any vain expectation in his heart, as to the reward awaiting his mission.[2]

The Lent of 1491 found him in the pulpit of Santa Maria del Fiore, the cathedral church of Florence, generally known as the Duomo, from the grand dome surmounting this splendid pile. The solemn grandeur of this stately edifice, of which Michaelangelo had said that, if smaller than St. Peter's in Rome, it was not less fair, was well adapted to the new preacher for whom San Marco's had proved too small. Lest the reader should infer that Savonarola's audience consisted chiefly of the "plain people," we deem it well to state that he had prudently anticipated the objections that scholars might bring against his reprobation of the immoral effects of merely pagan training. To meet the learned, whose false principles he had branded, and to prove that he spoke not from opposition to true culture, but in behalf of solid erudition and piety, he published several works that soon asserted their just influence over the leading literati, many of

---

2 "I entered the cloister," he said in one of his sermons, "to suffer; and when sufferings visited me I made a study of them, and they taught me to love always and to forgive always."

whom became his most attentive hearers in the Duomo. Hundreds, we are told, of the people rose at midnight, coming to the church, where they waited patiently for the opening of the doors. No inconvenience or suffering daunted them. They instinctively felt the goodness, the truth, of the friar who spoke to them, even in "terrible sermons;" they felt that he loved them, that he wished to keep them from going astray. Every manner of evil was condemned, but particularly the predominant sins of the day, —gambling, usury, avarice, revenge, impurity. At the same time, he exhorted his hearers to the practice of every virtue, inculcating with exceeding tenderness the duty of prayer, of charity, and of forgiveness of enemies.

The "contradictions" increased. Many thought religiously of the preacher's flaming words and renewed the spirit of their early faith; others considered the unhappy state of their city, robbed of her liberty, and hoped that the mighty reformer in religion would also aid in the struggle for civil freedom; while a third party, chiefly among the followers of Lorenzo, threatened to exile the bold stranger. These divided opinions caused a moment's hesitation on Savonarola's part as to the wisdom of discussing political affairs, or of announcing prophecies. However, after reflection, he resolved to continue. The Lenten course he finished under circumstances that evidenced the esteem in which he was held not only among the people, but among the nominal rulers of the city. Shortly after Easter, on the special invitation of the Signoria,[3] he appeared in the palace, and before their Excellencies delivered a stirring discourse on virtue in public officials and on the sins of tyrants. It was plain to all that Lorenzo was the man to whom the bold words of the preacher were directed nevertheless, "the Magnificent" took no measures against the friar. In July, 1491, Savonarola was elected Prior of San Marco's, he began his administration by enforcing stricter discipline among

---

3   Under this title is designated the supreme officials, or eight priors, chosen two from each quarter of the city, with one at their head who was known as the Gonfaloniere, or standard-bearer. They were elected for two months.

the Brethren. He also manifested his unyielding courage and in dependence by disregarding a custom which had previously been observed by newly elected priors during the Medicean regime—a visit to the prince, as an act of quasi-homage, and as a petition for his favour to the community. He refused to call on Lorenzo, sharply telling those who urged his going that it was to God and not to Lorenzo that he owed his election.

Then began a series of efforts on the part of "the Magnificent" to win over the man whom he considered a stranger in his house, but who would not stoop to pay him a visit. Apparently the first citizen of Florence recognized the mettle of the friar; nor could he deny to himself that such a man was worth winning, even if he were obliged to condescend to pay the stranger a visit.

Lorenzo was keener in his study of character than were the flatterers about him. He wished, if possible, to win the friendship of a man whom in his heart he admired, even though that man had both attacked and repulsed him. Accordingly, he went to San Marco's several times, and, having heard Mass, walked in the garden. It was natural that the Brethren should greet him and show him attention, for his grandfather had built their convent, and gratitude might be appropriately and with courtesy man-ifested to the grandson. Apprised of his presence, Savonarola demanded if Lorenzo had asked for him. Being informed that Lorenzo had not asked for him, he bluntly answered, "Then let him go or stay as he pleases." While admiring the spirit of Savon-arola, we are tempted to regret that he did not meet Lorenzo. Without any sacrifice of dignity this could have been effected, as Lorenzo had practically "gone half way."[4]

Though thus rebuffed, "the Magnificent" did not desist from his efforts to see the prior, to win him. Generous gifts were offered to San Marco's, and gold pieces were dropped into the Alms-box, to the surprise of the friars. They were further sur-

---

4   Perhaps the course of events might have been changed had these men first met then, and not, as the story goes, at Lorenzo's death-bed, and had they known each other more intimately.

prised when Savonarola sent all the gold to " the good men of St. Martin," a charitable organisation, and kept only the silver and copper for the Brethren. It must be admitted that the seeming bribe involved in this action of Lorenzo deserved reprobation if not contempt. He woefully misjudged the new prior, who, as he forcibly put it, would not be kept from barking because his master's enemy had thrown him a bone. Lorenzo next tried to influence Savonarola by sending to him a delegation of five distinguished citizens who had been instructed to speak as if they had gone of their own accord. They waited on the prior, and suggested to him the advisability of abstaining from political references in his sermons. They counselled him to moderate his style, for prudence and for the sake of his community. He listened, and then unhesitatingly told them that they did not speak for themselves, that they were only Lorenzo's messengers, to whom they should return with his answer: "I am a stranger, and I shall remain; Lorenzo is a citizen, even the first, but he must depart." It was on this occasion that he predicted, in the presence of several, the speedy deaths of Pope Innocent VIII, and of the Magnificent. The fulfilment of this prophecy added later to his fame.

Baffled by such determination and courage, Lorenzo resolved on a final stroke through which he hoped to accomplish the ruin of Savonarola in the public esteem. A certain Father Mariano, of the Augustinians, had attained some celebrity as an orator of the Florentine school. He was thoroughly classical. Lorenzo urged him to return to his pulpit, and Mariano at once responded. In the Church of San Gallo, on the feast of the Ascension, he announced as his text the seventh verse of the first chapter of the Acts of the Apostles: "It is not for you to know the times or moments, which the Father hath put in his own power." Building a vehement and harsh discourse on this text, he not only strove to carry out the suggestions of Lorenzo by denouncing recent prophecies, but he exceeded all reasonable bounds by attacking Savonarola as an impostor. Even Lorenzo heard him with dissatisfaction; others went away indignant and disgusted. Father Mariano lost his hard-won reputation; Savonarola, through a masterly answer, increased his fame and influence. Lorenzo made no further attempt either to harass or to win the indomitable Prior of San Marco's.[5]

5   It does not appear that common friends endeavoured to arrange a meeting between the two great men. If the attempt were made, it failed

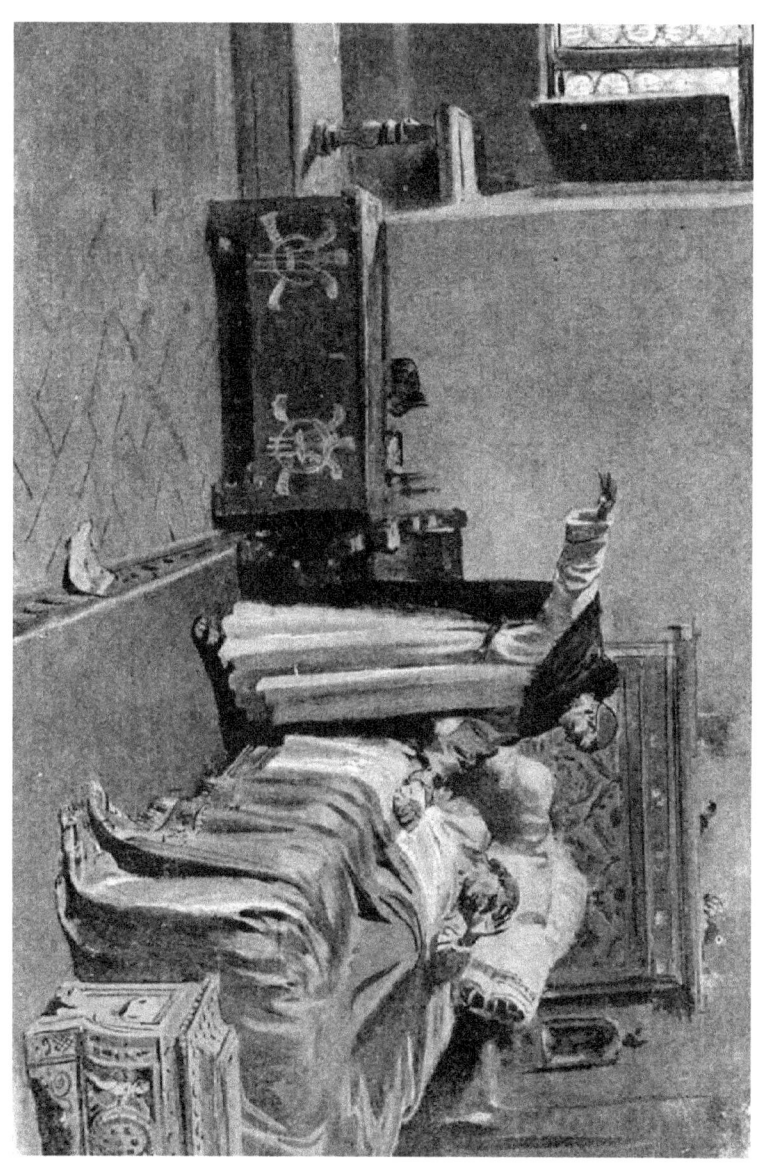

Savonarola at the deathbed of Lorenzo de' Medici.

VI

THE DEATH-BED OF LORENZO DE' MEDICI

✠

THE YEAR 1491 passed away without any other notable occurrence. In the spring of 1492, Lorenzo was prostrated by the disease that had for some time been making serious inroads on a constitution originally vigorous. Though only forty-four, the Magnificent felt that his end was drawing near. Then the Faith which had slumbered began to assert its influence; his heart, never hardened in evil, yielded. From scenes of carnival revelry, from the vanity of learning, from the music of his own songs, he turned away. Though he had already made a confession, he expressed a desire to see the Prior of San Marco's, and indeed sent a messenger, requesting Savonarola to visit him. The prior went, but with misgivings which he expressed.

Were it given to a historian or writer to read the hearts of those two men as Savonarola entered the apartment of Lorenzo, a picture vivid and dramatic might be drawn. For Lorenzo it was the supreme, because the closing moment of his career; for Savonarola it was an occasion demanding the fullest expression of his high moral courage, the exercise of the most delicate care, charity, and prudence.

With differences of detail that leave one in doubt, the scene in the chamber of Lorenzo, as prince and friar met for the first and last time on earth, is described by historians and biographers. We follow Burlamacchi: "Father, three sins especially burden me, and I desire to confess them, —the sack of Volterra, the robbery of the Monte delle Fanciulle and the massacres after the Pazzi conspiracy."[1]

"Lorenzo," Savonarola answered, "do not despair God is infinitely merciful, and to you will he show mercy if you will do three things."

"What are they?" the dying man asked.

"The first is that you must have a strong faith, believing that God can and will pardon you."

"I do believe," Lorenzo answered.

"You must also," the prior continued, "restore all ill-gotten goods, or impose on your sons the obligation of so doing."

Lorenzo hesitated, showed how keenly he felt this, but after a while agreed to the prior's demand.

"And lastly," said Savonarola, as he gazed solemnly and fixedly on the Magnificent, now so sorry a spectacle, "you must restore to Florence her liberty."

To this Lorenzo made no answer, only turning his face away. The stern friar then left the apartment.

There is much uncertainty as to the meaning and importance of this scene. As tragic, unmatched in history, some would paint it, investing with a living interest the episode of that spring morning more than four hundred years ago, when the Magnificent lay dying in his splendid villa among the beauties of nature and art that he had perhaps loved too well.

Even accepting Burlamacchi's account, and agreeing with Villari's estimate of its significance, we observe that it is not evident that Lorenzo sent for Savonarola for the purpose of con-

---

1   See Roscoe's *Life of Lorenzo de' Medici.*

fession. Certainly, no sacramental confession was made. Already Lorenzo had been absolved by another priest. May it not have been a desire on his part for reconciliation with the prior that prompted the dying man to send for him? Admitting, however, that Lorenzo intended to seek absolution from Savonarola, it is a question whether the latter's jurisdiction as a confessor extended to the matter of his third demand. Moreover, Lorenzo had his own right of conscience; and apparently, he maintained his own view when the matter was presented to him, for previously he did not refer to this phase of the interview, which was exclusively of Savonarola's suggestion and demand. Such an incident is available for word painting. Belonging, however, to the domain of conscience, and lacking the proofs necessary for the detailed circumstances of the visit, we prefer to pass it over in the silence of charity for the dying man, and without judgement as to Savonarola's rights and powers in the case.

VII

THE FRIAR'S VISIONS, JOURNEYS, LABORS—
REFORM OF THE CONVENTS
(1492-1494)

S AVONAROLA CONTINUED HIS sermons during 1492, increasing audiences testifying to his growing power and influence.[1] He had a fond love for the fair city of his adoption, and he longed to see her free; but it was the liberty of

[1] The reins that had fallen from the lifeless hands of Lorenzo were taken by Piero de' Medici, who inherited some of his father's good qualities, but these were not in the line of statesmanship. As a gallant and an athlete this young man might have achieved success, as the pilot of the vessel of state he was doomed to a miserable shipwreck. He alienated many of his father's staunch adherents, while he outraged the sensibilities of the citizens by ignoring some of the republican forms of liberty which, for the crafty deception of the people, had been preserved during Lorenzo's life. Moreover, the "contradictions" engendered among Savonarola's hearers became more bitter. Unfortunately, these factional divisions of the people seemed to mark him as- a mere party representative of those who were opposed to the Medici. Yet it may be justly said that no such position was deliberately assumed or desired by him, at least for mere political purposes. The immediate followers of Savonarola were generally known as the Piagnoni, or "Weepers." So we shall designate them. There were other factions known as the Biffii, or the "Greys" who favoured the Medici; the Bianchi, or the "Whites," an extreme group of the socialist or red republican brand; and the Arrabbiati, or the "Enraged," so called from their bitter opposition to Savonarola, and their fury against his sway.

the children of God, the fruit and crown of holy living, that he yearned for.[2]

His ardour for this work was further inflamed by two visions, which are recorded as having been vouchsafed to him during this year, the one in Lent, the other in Advent. From the city of Rome, on Good Friday night, he beheld a black cross rising to the heavens and extending its dread shadow over the world, while amid lightning and thunder the angry sky reflected back the words inscribed on the cross: "The Cross of the wrath of God." Immediately afterwards he saw a golden cross mounting from Jerusalem, filling the heavens with beautiful light, so that the worshipping world, as the peoples hastened to it, could clearly read the comforting words "The Cross of the mercy of God."

At the close of Advent, the second vision appeared to him. Distinct in the sky he beheld a hand grasping a naked sword, on which were inscribed the words: "The sword of the Lord will soon swiftly descend on the earth."

While the thunder peeled and the lightning flashed, and arrows and daggers seemed to fall on the world given over to rapine and bloodshed, he heard voices proclaiming mercy to the repentant, punishment to the obstinate, and bidding him warn the people that the Divine wrath might yet be averted.[3]

---

2   "God is essentially free, and the just man is free after the likeness of God. The only true liberty consists in the desire for righteousness. It seems to you that a good friar has no liberty, because he has submitted his will to that of others; but his freedom is greater than that of laymen exactly because he wills to do that which is commanded by others. "What liberty has he who is ruled by his passions? Now, in our case, O Florence! Do you desire liberty? Citizens, would you be free? First of all, love God, love your neighbour, love one another; seek the general welfare. If you have this love and union, true liberty will also be yours." These words, from one of Savonarola's sermons, embody the spirit and purpose of all his labours.

3   It is easy to realise how the announcement of such visions, apart from any question of their divine origin, must have affected the Florentines.

During 1492 the prior had visited Pisa on missionary labours, but his absences were brief. In 1493, however, he was assigned to Bologna as the Lenten preacher.[4]

Considerable success attended his efforts in Bologna but he was eager to return to Florence, where, as he had learned, affairs were in a perilous condition. At this time a change was effected that was of great importance to his work. After much difficulty he secured the separation of San Marco's from the Lombard jurisdiction of the Order. This step was taken in conformity with the laws of the Dominican Order, and as a return to the conditions existing previously to 1448, when the Tuscan convents formed an independent Congregation or Province. This Province of Tuscany was restored by the Holy See, and under its own Provincial was made subject directly to the Master General. Over this new division Savonarola was placed with full ordinary power. Piero had requested this change probably in deference to Tuscan sentiment, and without seeming to understand that it established Savonarola, as a resident of Florence, beyond the power of such removal as he had hitherto been subject to.

He organised the convents under his jurisdiction[5] according to strict discipline; and so great was the fervour of the Brethren of San Marco's, the centre of the reform, so strong had its attractions become, that the building was found inadequate for the accommodation of those who sought admission to the cloister. In a short time this community numbered more than two hundred friars, among whom not only was the study of phi-

---

4   It is charged by writers unfriendly to the Holy See that this was done at the instance of Piero de' Medici. Proof is lacking. The Dominican authorities were capable of administering their office without the intervention of the civil power. The writers who see politics in every event of Savonarola's life, as the mainspring of superiors' actions, only belittle the man and damage his cause by such insinuations.

5   The convent at Fiesole was among the first to join the reform movement. The community of Prato was transferred to the jurisdiction of the Tuscan Province by command of the Pope, who ordered the enforcement of the rule, under the direction of Savonarola. This action would indicate not only Alexander's acceptance of Savonarola's plea for the maintenance of his independent authority, but also the high regard of the Pontiff for the friar's religious spirit.

losophy and theology maintained at a high standard, but the arts were also assiduously cultivated. Savonarola likewise fostered missionary zeal in an eminently Apostolic spirit, so that San Marco's was truly the house of God and the home of Christian art and science.

In the Advent of 1493, Savonarola resumed his preaching in Florence, continuing during the Lent of 1494 the splendid discourses on faith, morals, and politics, or rather on the science of politics as founded in religion and conscience. These sermons included the famous series on Noah's Ark which he had commenced in 1492. Frequently during the year and a half that had elapsed from the death of Lorenzo till the autumn of 1494, Savonarola had announced to the people the coming of a new Cyrus, who, as a scourge, would be the instrument of the Divine Justice. On Sept. 21st he spoke on the Deluge. The Duomo was crowded with an expectant multitude. The preacher's words were as fire. When simultaneously with the thunder of Savonarola's eloquence, the terrible tidings spread that the French King was crossing the Alps to invade Italy, the Florentines were, more than ever, perturbed.

VIII

PATRIOTISM OF THE FRIAR DURING THE FRENCH INVASION

✠

TO MAKE CLEAR this episode in Savonarola's career a brief explanation is necessary of the political complications which occasioned the expedition of Charles VIII of France, an event which, as Machiavelli wrote, "ruined Italy, and kept her in desolation;" and, as Gibbon declared, "changed the face of Europe." Of this invasion Villari writes that it "proved to be the beginning of the long series of disasters which were to desolate Italy for ages, to destroy her commercial prosperity, to stifle her literary and scientific culture, and to extinguish every spark of her liberty."

A benefactor to all Europe, the eyes of Italy's neighbours were turned in eagerness and avarice on this fair domain of culture, wealth, and power. The growing states of Europe were ready, from motives of greed and conquest, from the very spirit of restlessness and brigandage pervading the royal and noble robbers of those days, to act against weaker powers. Italy was weak because of her divisions. Among the Italian states the lordship of Milan was then held by Ludovico Sforza, surnamed the Moor. This unprincipled man, the guardian of his minor nephew, the rightful Duke of Milan, usurped the place of his charge, imprisoned him, and it is alleged, poisoned him. The young duke had married the daughter of the King of Naples, who naturally resented the cruel treatment of his daughter and her husband. The anger of this monarch, the usurper dreaded, as he also feared the just indignation of other Italian rulers.

After attempting various schemes, he resolved to secure for himself a powerful ally by urging Charles of Anjou, King of France, to come to Italy and claim, though on a baseless title, the Neapolitan throne. Charles came, with sixty thousand men, and calamity followed his march. Savonarola saw in the French monarch another Cyrus, an instrument of justice and of punishment.

Respecting Florence, however, events took a turn most embarrassing and disadvantageous to the Republic. The party opposed to Piero desired the coming of the king, in the hope that the Medici might be expelled. Piero adopted a policy of opposition to Charles, but failed to sustain it by any decided action. He excited the king's anger, and then foolishly hastened to put himself in Charles's power by surrendering, without any compensation, three of Tuscany's most important fortresses. He also promised, in return for the royal protection, to raise a large sum of money for Charles. These actions angered the Florentines. As a visitor passing through their territory they would have welcomed the French monarch but his coming as an enemy, that would not be placated even by Piero's surrender of their fortresses and promised gift of money, terrified them. At this juncture, while the French king was yet distant from the city, Florentine ambassadors followed Piero, hoping to make honourable terms with Charles, but he put them off with vain words.

These events occurred early in November. The French were then on Florentine territory, and by the force of their numbers and military equipment, Tuscany lay helpless before them. In the meantime, the rumours of their advance had reached Florence, where a scene of disorder and riotous murder would have been the natural result among an enraged people who believed they had been betrayed by their incompetent and cowardly "first citizen." At this moment of extreme peril Savonarola was the one man to whom all the citizens looked. While the Signoria held counsel with men of repute and patriotism, the prior ascended the pulpit of the Duomo. His spirit seemed to penetrate the vast assembly as he stretched over them his hands, and solemnly announced to them that the time had come for repentance, now that his prophecies were fulfilled.

Over hearts seething with anger and vengeance, over minds devising ways and means of executing speedy justice on the Medici, God's grace and light fell, through the preacher's marvellous discourse; and the mighty throng went out from the Duomo, filled with a spirit of forgiveness towards their enemies, and with the patient courage that marks true patriotism. Savonarola had saved Florence from scenes of blood and rapine.[1] The work of the Signoria was thus rendered comparatively easy. Instead of a revolutionary mob, they found a practically united people, ready to face the difficulties and dangers that threatened.

Though preparing for defence, the Florentines deemed it advisable to send another embassy to Charles. Of this body Savonarola was a member. He did not, however, accompany the citizens who had been commissioned with him, but following them, in the company of some of his brethren, he went out to meet the French king, who was encamped at Pisa. During Savonarola's absence on this embassy the indignant Florentines expelled Piero de' Medici (who had returned to the city), and

---

1   "It would be well," writes Dr. Clark, "for those who think of the friar as a wild fanatic eager for power, burning with hatred against the Medici, and unscrupulous in his denunciations of the enslavers of Florence, to study his conduct at this crisis. One word from him and the city would have been given up to revolt and confusion. One word from him, and the palace of the Medici and all its treasures would have perished forever." The power and goodness of the prior were felt by Cardinal de' Medici, who brought many of the family valuables and placed them in his care at San Marco's.

his brother, the Cardinal, afterwards Pope Leo the Tenth. The lay ambassadors accomplished little with the French. Charles would make no promises beyond a general declaration that all would be arranged after his entrance into the city. On the arrival of Savonarola, of whose prophecies concerning himself Charles had heard, the monarch granted speedy audience to the friar. The accounts of this interview differ in details, but on essential points the historians are agreed. It was a picturesque scene. Savonarola spoke fearlessly, telling the most Christian king that, as the messenger of God, he greeted him who came as the instrument of God, to punish the guilty and to protect the innocent. "Nevertheless," he continued, "hearken to the warning of God's unworthy servant. For the sake of the many just and virtuous who are in Florence, spare that city. Reform the abuses which afflict God's Church. If these things are done, thy kingdom will be increased. But if thou dost neglect the work which the Lord hath called thee to do, another will be set in thy place, and His wrath will scourge thee. These things I declare to thee in the name of the Lord." The king did not commit himself, though seemingly moved by Savonarola's address. The latter returned to Florence, bringing comfort to the people even by his presence, though he bore messages scarcely more satisfactory than those of the other ambassadors. Charles would arrange no terms for an understanding or treaty with the Florentines until lie had passed through their gates.

On November 17th, many of his officers having previously arrived, the French monarch was received with pomp by the Signoria, who had provided for him and his immediate suite in the splendid Medici palace. The visit lasted ten days, and during this time Charles proved himself to be a troublesome as well as a dishonest guest. Previous to the ratification of a treaty, which had been the occasion of much dispute, the arrogant monarch showed a disposition to act harshly, threatening even to sack the city.

Again were Savonarola's efforts successful among the people for the preservation of peace, and for the avoidance of strife or collision with the foreign troops who were scattered through the city. Once more he brought his personal influence to bear directly on the king. Having sought the royal presence, without introduction or hesitation he bluntly told Charles that his Majesty's stay was causing great injury to the people and the city, as well as to the work which God had imposed on him, reproaching him for losing valuable time.[2] He urged Charles to pursue his journey without further delay, or his worldly fame, as well as his spiritual interests, would suffer. He concluded by threatening the king with the wrath of God if he inflicted any injury on the city. These brave words had the desired effect. Charles resumed his march, carrying with him, however, despite the generous treatment he had received, many art treasures that had been collected by the Medici. As the royal plunderer had numerous imitators among officers and soldiers, it is not surprising that the indignation and hatred of the Florentines followed the French army on its way to Naples.

2   We quote Savonarola's words, without passing any judgement as to his views of the campaign of the French king.

Portrait of Piero de' Medici by Gherardo di Giovanni del Fora (1494).

IX

✠

I F SAVONAROLA'S SERVICES to the Florentines had been of inestimable value during the troublous days of the French visit, when the grateful love of the people had loudly proclaimed their debt to the prior, the assistance he rendered subsequently was not of less importance. Great confusion prevailed, in consequence of the expulsion of Piero de' Medici, whose "reign" in the "Republic" closed sixty years of Medicean rule, under which the foundations of liberty had been destroyed, a mere semblance of liberty having been preserved by the continuance of certain forms and names, from which all spirit and living meaning had departed. A strong government was needed, and the friends of Florentine freedom realised that vigorous measures must be adopted.

Among a people of high temper and ardent spirit, passing through such a crisis, there was special need of a prudent and clear-sighted leader. Savonarola did not assume that post; events determined it for him. Many looked to him as the man of the hour, providentially set for a great work. He was not only faithful to expectations that had been aroused, but by his sermons, his entreaties to the rich to be generous, to the poor to be patient, to employers to provide opportunities for labour, to all to practise mutual charity, to be faithful in prayer and piety, he established the temporary empire of religion over Florence, and wonderfully smoothed the way for political reconstruction, in which, as yet, he had taken no direct part. But as Villari well says, "The hour had struck for his appearance in the arena of politics, and notwithstanding the firm determination with which he had hitherto held aloof from it, he was now compelled to obey the summons by the pressure of events."[1]

The appearance of Savonarola in the political arena as the champion of liberty is an event significant in itself, though the history of Florence, and Italian history in general, furnish many notable instances of saintly men, and even women, who entered into the public life of their day for the betterment of civil affairs. On two points his most severe critics must render homage to the truth (1) Savonarola was a preacher, a religious, a priest of holiness beyond dispute, waiving his relations with Alexander VI; (2) Savonarola was the moral and political regenerator of Florence.

Disinterested, unselfish, his big, brave heart was filled with love for the people, with solicitude for the welfare of the poor, with zeal for the salvation of souls. No thought of winning political power was his; he simply used the rich gifts with which God had endowed him, as he felt divinely urged, to speak and act for the people.[2]

On the third Sunday of Advent, 1494, his sermon indicated the trend of his thoughts on affairs of state. He laid the foundation deep in religion, love of God, mercy and charity towards all, forgiveness of enemies, forgetfulness of past injuries and

1   For an account of the cumbrous method of Florentine political administration, see Villari's *Life and Times of Jerome Savonarola*; Symonds's *Age of the Despots*; or the histories of Florence and Italy mentioned in our Appendix.

2   No material interest of San Marco's Convent or of the Church in general influenced his conduct. Rather, he cried out, "Cease from building churches; yea, the very gold and silver of the sanctuary convert into money that the poor may be fed, and I shall lead the way."

wrongs, the pardon and restoration of those who had been identified with Piero. He pleaded for such a government as would best assure the interest of all, and best serve the welfare of the public as against that of individuals. He urged a rectification of taxes, a more equitable distribution of these burdens among the rich and the poor. Finally he recommended the formation of a Grand Council, after the manner of the Venetians. Within two weeks the political measures which he had outlined were carried into effect. Out of a helpless, almost chaotic condition, the friar had evolved order; he had suppressed civil rebellion, and held in check a most excitable people. To lawyers and men versed in politics he gave such a lesson in statecraft that all were amazed at his practical knowledge of public affairs.

Only one measure that he recommended was doomed to failure. He urged the formation of a select court of last resort as a check on the arbitrary power of the bench of judges, who were known as "The Eight." Savonarola's wise suggestion was not adopted. The court was not established, though the right of appeal was admitted to the Grand Council, a body numbering several thousand. Though only one-third of this body acted at a time, and for a given period, it was too unwieldy for the delicate and deliberative responsibilities contemplated by Savonarola. He recommended the establishment of the *Monte di Pieta*[3] for the temporary relief of the deserving poor by loans at moderate interest, thus freeing thousands from the clutches of the usurers, whose system of compounding interest was a legalised method of robbery.[4]

During the closing days of 1494 the Republic was re-established, the result being largely the achievement of the prior, to whom nearly all had turned in the hour of peril. The work

3   Pious Banks, —a free rendering.

4   This generous service to the people aroused the anger of the money-changers, adding to the political enemies of Savonarola a combination of bankers and usurers who continued in their pursuit of vengeance till his downfall was accomplished. The modern pawn-shop is the evolution, by a downward progress and with disregard of religion, of the mediaeval Monte di Pieta.

was rapidly developed. By the end of 1495 the people enjoyed liberty to such a degree that the government never more truly deserved the name of Republic. The city had been transformed. Indeed, Savonarola had proclaimed from the pulpit the freedom of the children of God, under the kingship of Jesus Christ over all hearts, and in a sense, it may be said that he established a Theocracy in the city where pagan ideas and manners had so lately reigned. Vice no longer stalked unrebuked in the streets; rather had the reign of virtue been inaugurated. Were secret excesses diminished? Should youth be denied moderate amusements? These questions conservative men put one to another in Savonarola's day. It is to be feared that the city passed too rapidly from one extreme to the other, and that Savonarola encouraged among an unprepared multitude the application of principles in details available only for the cloister.

X

THE FRIAR SAVES FLORENCE FROM THE FRENCH KING

✠

DURING 1495 SAVONAROLA was unflagging in the work of preaching. At the beginning of the year a serious difficulty confronted him through the machinations of the *Arrabbiati*. These men sought the downfall of the Republic, in the hope of erecting on its ruins an aristocracy or oligarchy. Through their misrepresentations, the Pope was induced to order Savonarola to proceed to Lucca. The prior made ready to leave, but the Signoria and many others, by most urgent letters, prevailed on His Holiness to reconsider his command. Savonarola remained in Florence. Before the opening of his regular Lenten course, he preached several sermons, one of notable force and vehemence, in which ecclesiastical disorders and the sins of princes were unsparingly rebuked. The publication of this discourse, known as the "renewal sermon," was an occasion of bitter strife. His followers hailed it with delight. The *Arrabbiati* circulated it for the harm they hoped it would bring on the preacher, through the animosity of those in high places against whom he had so strongly spoken.

How far this incident influenced the tone of Savonarola's discourses during Lent we know not, but a sadness and gloom pervaded them. He frequently referred to the violent death that already, he seemed clearly to foresee. Another event that sorely tried Savonarola's soul was the attempt made by his enemy, the Gonfaloniere Corbizzi, to have him condemned for interference in affairs of state. For this purpose Corbizzi summoned a council of theologians to the palace. Among them was a decided opponent of Savonarola, in fact, his most obstinate assailant, a Dominican named Thomas of Rieti, a member of the community of Santa Maria Novella.

Having heard the charges, Savonarola, to whom the purpose of the meeting had not previously been known (for he was accustomed to preach occasionally before the Signoria), made a noble answer, first sharply scoring his Dominican opponent, and then completely confounding the others by his dexterous defence.[1] However, this action of the Gonfaloniere showed that the tide was turning against Savonarola, though the people still remained devoted to the friar, and though many of the influential men of the city were his most ardent admirers.

Worn by anxieties and labours, and by a rigid discipline, Savonarola finished his Lenten sermons under extraordinary stress. The city took on a new life. Everywhere signs abounded of the reformation that had taken place. Multitudes thronged the confessionals: restitution was made on a large scale by those who held unjust gains alms for the poor were abundant; the practice of prayer and spiritual reading and the singing of

---

1   "In me," he said, "is fulfilled that saying of the Lord, '*Flii matris meae pug-naverunt contra me,*' — 'My mother's children have fought against me'; yet it grieves me to see that my fiercest opponent wears the habit of St. Dominic. That habit should remind him that our Founder involved himself not a little in the things of this world; that from our Order have gone forth saints and religious who have concerned themselves in the doings of the state. Will the Republic of Florence remember Cardinal Latino, St. Peter Martyr, St. Catherine of Siena, St. Antoninus, who all belonged to the Order of St. Dominic? It is not concerning ourselves with the doings of this world in which God has placed us that should be condemned in a religious, but it is doing so without having regard to a higher end, without an eye to the good of religion."

hymns gave a conventual air to the domestic hearth; ribaldry and licentiousness among the reckless young men of the city were renounced; pomp and vanity among the rich and lordly gave way to Christian modesty and simplicity. Savonarola was a reformer, but Catholic to the core in all the changes he wrought, though erring on the score of over-strictness. All classes were amenable to his influence. From distant places many came, women and men, to hear the far-famed prior. The noblest families of Florence gave a strong proof of their veneration for Savonarola in the free surrender of their sons to enter the Dominican Order as his followers.

The changes he wrought in the customs of the people invited opposition, and this was supplied by the *Arrabbiati* who persistently waged a war fare of petty spite against him. They hurled nicknames at the *Piagnoni* at all who held him in reverence, and sneeringly spoke of them as "toadies," "prayer-mumblers," "twisted necks." But as Villari pointedly says,

> The Piagnoni were the only determined defenders of the people's rights, the readiest to fly to arms when Florence was threatened by the French, the most generous in giving money to the state, and in tenderly succouring the poor who were suffering from the high price of food and scarcity of work. Their devotion to the Republic was the more tenacious because liberty and religion were as one in their and in all public emergencies it was only hearts;[2] on these followers of the friar that the country could really depend.

2   Mr. Symonds claims that the Piagnoni were the backbone of the Florentine people, those who might have saved the state had a political salvation been possible for it.

XI

REFORMATION OF THE PEOPLE INSPITE OF OPPOSITION

✠

CHARLES VIII PROVED untrue to his pledged word, to the treaty made with the Florentines, to the best purpose to which Savonarola had entreated his devoted loyalty as an instrument of God. The end of May found him, accompanied by Piero de' Medici, at Siena, on his return journey from the disastrous Neapolitan campaign. There he was met by ambassadors from Florence who desired to learn the line of his march. His treatment of them was insolent and threatening. Again the aid of Savonarola was invoked. The letter which he addressed to the French monarch is a noble document; it proclaims the power and courage of the friar:

> Most Christian Sire, —It is the Lord's will that the Florentines should continue their alliance with your Majesty; but He wishes your protection to extend the freedom of the people, not of any individual, for God has ordained the fall of all tyrants. The Lord will inflict terrible punishment on any private citizen who seeks to usurp, as in the past, the government of this flourishing Republic, which has been constituted, not by man, but by God. He has chosen this city to increase it. He has filled it with His servants;

whosoever touches it touches the apple of His eye. Therefore, Sire, if you will not obey Him by keeping your pledges to the Florentines, and restoring their fortresses, many calamities will come upon you, and nations will rise against you.

In a few days Savonarola followed this letter by going out to Poggibonsi, where the king had advanced. Again he spoke as the messenger of God, boldly telling Charles that his disobedience to God was the cause of his failure and losses. Savonarola further declared that the king had provoked the Divine anger by his treachery to the Florentines, and by his refusal to effect the reforms for which God had called him. He concluded his address by warning him for the last time that, if he did not earnestly take up the work of God, still greater calamities would come upon him, and God would reject him. Charles no further annoyed the city of Florence. His ill-concealed friendliness for the Pisans, then in revolt against Florence, and his retention of the fortresses which Piero had so pusillanimously surrendered to him, occasioned, however, heavy loss and trouble to the Republic, while his encouragement of Piero emboldened the expelled prince to attempt a forcible entrance of the city.

This attempt failed, but it occasioned a manifestation of patriotism and courage on the part of the Florentines and their spiritual leader deserving the highest praise. Savonarola's sermons at this time—October—were marked by a vigour and fire that some have considered excessive. But they do not justly weigh his words who separate them from the conditions and dangers out of which they sprang. As a true patriot Savonarola spoke.

Portrait of Pope Alexander VI Borgia attributed to Pedro Berruguete (circa 1495).

XII

Relations with the Pope
(1495)

✠

THE OPINION OF certain writers that Florence's opposition to the league of Italian states,[1] of which the Pope
was a member, irritated and angered Alexander VI
against Savonarola, we ought not to attach undue importance.
Admitting that the friar's political attitude was offensive to the
Pope, other circumstances were conspiring to draw the Pontiff's
attention to the preacher. His sermons, in which ecclesiastical
abuses were unsparingly lashed, were reported, perhaps in an
exaggerated form, and were sent to Rome, with inflammatory
letters from his persistent enemies in Florence. The sovereign
Pontiff was obliged to take notice of a man who had made powerful enemies among prelates of high rank, and who had become
the storm centre, politically and ecclesiastically, of the day. The
following letter was despatched to the Prior of San Marco's, by
Alexander, on July 25th, 1495:

> Beloved son,
>
> Health and Apostolic Blessing. Amongst the many

[1] For the expulsion of the barbarians, as the French were called.

who have laboured in the vineyard of the Lord we
have learned from several sources that your labours
have been especially earnest and successful. This
fills us with deep joy and gratitude to God, Who so
powerfully works among us by His grace. Nor do we
doubt but that you are an instrument in His hands
for the abundant sowing of His Divine word, and the
reaping of a plentiful harvest. However, recent letters
on this very subject have given us to understand that
in all your sermons you instruct the people in the service of God, and that you announce future events,
being moved thereto, not by human learning or wisdom, but by the Spirit of God. Being desirous, therefore, as is our duty, of conferring with you on these
matters, and so learning God's will more clearly, we
wish you to come to us as soon as possible, and we
give you a command in virtue of holy obedience to
that effect. We shall greet you with all fatherly tenderness and love.

Recalling what travel meant in those days, and considering
the necessary slowness and uncertainty of mail delivery, we can
understand that there may have been no needless delay in Savonarola's answer, which is dated July 31st:

Most Holy Father,

I prostrate myself at the feet of your Holiness. Although I am aware that we must always obey the
commands of our superiors, since we read in Holy
Writ, "he that heareth you, heareth Me," still it is
their meaning and not merely their words that we
have to obey. And because I have long desired to visit Rome, and to worship at the shrine of the Apostles, to venerate the relics of so many saints, and to
see your Holiness, these ardent longings have greatly
increased since I received the letter of your Holiness
deigning to invite one so unworthy to your presence.
But as there are many difficulties in the way, I shall
humbly lay them before your Holiness, so that you
may see the reasonableness of my excuses, and that
it is necessity and not unwillingness which prevents
me from obeying the command which I received,
with the deepest love and reverence. In the first place,

there is the delicate state of my health, the result of fever and other sickness which I have had of late. Then my position here, especially during the past year, has entailed on me such a continual strain of mind and body that I am exceedingly weak, utterly unable to undertake any work, or to bear the least fatigue. The physicians have obliged me to give up all study and preaching, for in their opinion and in that of many friends, I shall endanger my life, unless I at once submit to proper treatment. Moreover, since Almighty God has made use of me to deliver this city from bloodshed and other serious evils, and to establish peace with respect for law, I have made as many enemies as there are wicked men in this place; for whether they are citizens or strangers, they vented their rage on me when they saw their love for fighting, their ambition, and their greedy thoughts of rapine and plunder frustrated. At the present moment their plots against my life, either by open assassination or secret poisoning, are so frequent that I cannot leave the house without guards. Indeed, when I went to confer with the French King the loyal Florentines would not allow me to pass out of their protection, although I was furnished with a safe-conduct. Although I trust in God, I must not despise ordinary precautions, lest I should seem to tempt Him, since it is written, "when they persecute you in one city, flee into another." Moreover, the recent improvement in this city which God's grace has effected, is hardly sufficiently established to withstand the persistent efforts of the wicked and needs daily care and attention. Since, therefore, my departure at the present moment would, in the opinion of earnest and prudent men, cause difficulties among the people, and help the plots of the Medicean faction, it is evidently not God's will that I should leave here at present. I hope it will he soon. And if, perhaps, your Holiness wishes to know more about the misfortunes of Italy and the renovation of the Church, of which I have publicly spoken, it is all fully treated in a book which I am now having printed, and which, as soon as it is ready, I shall send to your Holiness. From it you will be able to gather all you wish to hear. I have said nothing that is not there. I have only delivered

the message entrusted to me. To go beyond that,
and to attempt to read the unknown secrets of God,
would be sinful. I have had these things printed that
all may know if I have been deceived or deceiving.
But if things happen, as I have said, then let them
thank our Lord and Saviour, Who by His loving care
of us, shows that He wishes no one to perish eternal-
ly. And therefore, I ask your Holiness to accept these
my excuses as most true and valid, and to believe that
nothing could give me greater joy than to be able to
carry out your commands. I need no other spur than
my own desire to urge me to conquer these difficulties as soon as I can, and to satisfy the wishes of your
Holiness to whom I commend myself in all humility.

The tenor of the Pope's letter is indulgent, benign, and gentle.
Villari contends that the Brief was issued in a spirit of deceit,
to entrap Savonarola, but he offers no proof. Rather are the
circumstances and the evidence against this aspersion of the
Pope's motives.

Savonarola's old antagonist, Mariano, was at that time in
Rome, and Villari contends that his rabid and calumnious discourses had embittered Alexander. We are of the opinion that
His Holiness had weightier cares than listening to the complaints and dissensions of friars. Villari also maintains that the
Arrabbiati were plotting against Savonarola, and that a journey
to Rome at that time, literally among thieves and murderers,
might have been attended by assassination on the way, or by life-
long imprisonment at the end. With this conclusion we cannot
entirely agree. Moreover, we may not interpret the mind of the
Pope beyond his written words, and they are fatherly. Politics
probably entered into the question, but the command of the
Pope was the supreme law for Savonarola. However, as Alexander had set no time for his visit to Rome, and as commands
are amenable to a reasonable construction when their terms are
vague, the friar's prompt excuses expressed in the respectful
language which we have quoted, may have been justified. Previously to answering the Pontiff's letter, Savonarola announced

his withdrawal from the pulpit, on account of his illness, the shattered state of his health, and the exhaustion evident to all.

To the casual reader, Savonarola's letter suggests a want of frankness, together with an assumption of judgement, scarcely compatible with that obedience which is due to a superior. On this point we remark that some authors deem this letter justified by Savonarola's intense conviction, not only from a certain conscience, the rule of morals, but from the heavenly light which he believed had been vouchsafed to him, and which he interpreted as imposing an imperative duty upon him. With this view we cannot coincide; even admitting such an interpretation, it would show, on Savonarola's part, excessive zeal, for which there may be alleviation, but not entire justification, even under the extraordinarily trying circumstances attending Savonarola's difficulty with the Pope. Still, we hold that his spirit was of obedience, and the tacit acceptance of his excuses by Alexander would indicate that the Pontiff did not then consider the friar wanting in submission. His closing discourse at the end of July he called a "terrible" sermon; yet, as was his wont it was stamped with the spirit of tenderness for the people, and gentleness towards sinners, a spirit that went out even to the hated Jews, at a time when other ecclesiastics had demanded severe measures against them. Truly broken in health, Savonarola retired to San Marco's, and Father Dominic of Pescia, his faithful disciple, took his place in the pulpit of the Duomo.

Scarcely six weeks had elapsed when a second brief was issued by the Pope.[2] Though intended for Savonarola and San Marco's,

2   Here we may remark that the complaints addressed to the Holy See were not by politicians alone; churchmen of various grades joined in the cry against the daring preacher who had been go unsparing of denunciation against irregularities clergy, both secular and religious, refused absolution to those of their penitents who attended the friar's sermons. Thus the ecclesiastical animosities which existed in those days were not merely the ebullitions of passing human temper, signs of human frailty; they were, in a manner, an unfortunate outgrowth of the prevailing evils against which Savonarola had thundered. As Pico della Mirandola writes, "when the fame of his holiness grew, with it envy grew, and from envy came calumnies; for as his virtues won for him friends, so did they raise up enemies. Amongst his most bitter foes were those prelates of the Church, some of them, who by their evil lives were giving scandal." "He had preached against them," says the English

this Brief was addressed to the friars of the Holy Cross Church who had been opponents of the Dominicans. It referred to the prior of San Marco's as a "certain friar Jerome, a seeker after novelty and a disseminator of false doctrines," claiming to have a Divine mission, but without proof of Holy Writ or miracles. The Brief then branched off on the subject of the Lombard jurisdiction (the separation from which Alexander himself had authorised for San Marco's), branding as scandalous the position held by Savonarola and the brethren of San Marco's, several of whom were summarily ordered to Bologna. Savonarola was directed to show himself subject to the superior of the Lombard Congregation and to hold himself ready for a summons by that prelate to whom (though a party to the previously settled dispute) the affair was now referred for final judgement.

We may pass over the circumstance that the Brief was addressed to another community, on the supposition that this would guarantee publicity, though no action or word of Savonarola or his brethren had as yet given any occasion for holding them under the suspicion that they would suppress the Brief. The reference to a "certain friar Jerome," in the face of Alexander's previous personal letter to him, is puzzling; it may have been the work of one of the Pope's secretaries. The charge of false doctrine was subsequently stamped as false, even in Alexander's day, and more emphatically, by one of his successors. The sudden interjection of a question of jurisdiction between two provinces of the Order, a matter which Alexander himself had decided, and to which in his former letter he made no reference, suggests to Villari a religious pretext for picking a political quarrel; but the inference is not clear. Savonarola was in a sore dilemma. On either horn he might be impaled. That he was grievously troubled and yet seemingly unshaken in the sense of religious duty, we

---

Dominican, Father Procter; "he had spoken openly of their sins; he had said with the Baptist: 'It is not lawful.' Like Herodias, they would be content with nothing but his head, — and his head they received." Concerning the Pontifical letter dated the eighth of September, it is necessary to explain certain peculiarities so that the whole may be placed in a proper light.

gather from a letter addressed by him to one of the Dominicans in Rome:[3]

> All the world knows that the charges against me are false. My accusers have no cause for attack; rather they stone me for a good deed. But I neither dread them nor fear their power, for I rely on the grace of God and an upright conscience. I know who the real authors of these troubles are. They are wicked citizens who desire to raise themselves to power, and their accomplices are wicked princes of Italy. They all wish to rid themselves of my presence here, at any cost, since they consider me an obstacle to their ambition. In fact, I dare not leave the convent without an escort. If His Holiness knew all, I do not think that he would wish me to go to Rome. I will obey, however, even though my obedience should bring about the ruin of the world, for I would not sin, even venially, in this affair.

Comment on these sentiments would be superfluous. In his answer to the Pope, sent towards the end of the same month, he respectfully defended his doctrines, denied that he had ever claimed absolutely to be a prophet, reminded Alexander how the separation of San Marco's from the Lombard jurisdiction had been effected, on the appeal of the entire community, submitted all his writings to the judgement of the Holy See, and declared his prompt readiness to accept the correction and guidance of the Church. To this letter Alexander replied on the sixteenth of October, though Savonarola did not receive the papal Brief for several weeks. In this communication Alexander praised the obedience of Savonarola, admitted his good intentions but commanded him to desist from further preaching till he would be able, with honour and safety, to make the journey to Rome. Savonarola complied with this injunction against his preaching, Father Dominic taking his place in the Cathedral, during the succeeding Advent.

---

3   Savonarola's expressions, "all the world," "no cause for attack," "all wish to rid themselves," etc., must be taken in a rhetorical sense

XIII

REFORMATION OF THE CHILDREN OF FLORENCE
(1495-1496)

✠

THE CLOSING DAYS of 1495 found Savonarola in retirement, but active with his pen. Though enfeebled in health, his mind had lost none of its clearness, nor was his high spirit daunted. Sharing the opinion held by many of the cardinals, as well as by a large number of bishops, priests, and laymen, who were zealous for the honour of religion, Savonarola longed for the assembling of a Council. He wrote to Charles of France, and urged this hesitating monarch to take steps towards the desired end. He also engaged in other correspondence, but always bearing on the spiritual life. The time for the Carnival of 1496 was approaching, and it was evident that the *Arrabbiati* were determined to restore the abominable features which had prevailed in the Medicean days. Savonarola resolved to prevent this, though he knew full well the disposition of the people, and the readiness with which they could be swayed back to the sins they had abandoned. Their conversion was not lasting; rather, a passing emotion momentarily changed them. Knowing this, he would not have been surprised by any outburst of wickedness among those who had been swayed only by that wonderful voice, now no longer ringing out the threats of Divine Justice, or gently urging the pleadings of Divine mercy. He began his campaign with the boys. He inaugurated the "reform of the children." In this work we find a most interesting phase of Savonarola's mission. For generations the Florentines had been accustomed to revelry and even debauchery (especially under the Medici) during Carnival holidays. The boys took part in the celebration in a way characteristic of youthful heedlessness and even of cruelty. A game they played at this time was known as that of the stones, a brutal and occasionally fatal "pastime" which closed the day's festivities. After having secured means for a supper by intercepting the people on the street, whose passage they would not allow except on the payment of money, the evening was spent around a huge "bonfire." At this time they found entertainment in pelting one another with stones. Against these disorderly customs, warnings, threats, and penalties, had proved ineffective.

The great preacher, silenced, deprived of the privilege of exercising his marvellous God-given power in the pulpit, took to heart the case of the children whose improvement was not beneath the effects of the man who had politically and morally reformed their elders. And his success was pronounced. Catering to the military and political instinct that is quick in the heart of every *"real"* boy, Savonarola marshalled the Florentine youth (the same wild, lovable fellows in the fifteenth century that we find in the nineteenth), according to the "quarters" of the city, and had them elect their own captains, with counsellors for the captains. Thus organised, he exhorted them to make a new carnival. For the shameful songs that they had sung, would they not sing the new songs? He himself would write them, and fitting music would also be provided. We seem to hear the honest-hearted boys, who felt that the great prior was their true friend, as they promised to sing his hymns. And the worn preacher kindled again the poetic fires of other days, and forgetting the triumphs of the Duomo, burying in his own great heart his sorrows and his wrongs wrote for the lads sweet hymns and pure songs whose sacred melody would rise to Heaven in reparation for the shameful ballads of Medicean days.

He allowed the boys to beg, but not offensively, not to the intercepting of any passerby. From house to house they went; and when at night they had gathered a rich harvest, and it was turned over to the "Good Men of St. Martin" for the modest and deserving poor, beyond doubt the generous and tender-hearted prior made ample provision for a big supper for his Florentine boys. Here we may anticipate, to mention Savonarola's special solicitude for the children during the Lent of 1496, when he also arranged a novel and most interesting procession on Palm Sunday. His success with the boys during the Carnival assured his further success in the Palm Sunday celebration. The *Monte di Pieta* to which we have already referred, had been for some time in operation. Desirous of assisting still further in this meritorious work, he instituted a procession of the children, who visited all the churches, sang hymns, collected alms, and, at the close, made a handsome offering to the pious work. "And so much joy was there in all hearts" says Burlamacchi, "that the glory of Paradise seemed to have descended on earth, and many tears of tenderness and devotion were shed." Who can wonder that under the impulse of these extraordinary changes, the Florentines cried out "Live Jesus Christ, our King!"

Statue of Savonarola by Enrico Pazzi in Florence. Photograph by Alexander Norton.

XIV

A New Course of Sermons Awakens Papal Displeasure

✠

W
E MUST RETURN to the early winter of 1496, when the choice of a Lenten preacher was uppermost in the minds of Savonarola's friends. Through their persistent efforts they succeeded in securing permission from Pope Alexander that he might resume his sermons. He was immediately chosen to speak in the Duomo during the entire Lent.[1] The holy season opened with the Cathedral thronged,

---

1 An event of uncertain date is ascribed to this time. Alexander commissioned a Dominican bishop, whose name is not recorded, to examine the published sermons of Savonarola. This prelate reported to His Holiness that not only were there no theological flaws in the friar's writings, but that on the contrary his teaching was wise and just. The suggestion was also made by this bishop that it would be prudent for the Pope to win the friendship of Savonarola by offering to him a cardinal's hat. Here again exact dates are wanting; but the fact seems established that Alexander did approach the friar, through another Dominican, who had been authorised to communicate the Pope's intention of enrolling him among the members of the Sacred College. This, we may believe, was intended as a reward for the virtues and services of the great preacher, generously recognized by the Pontiff. Alexander's enemies among the advocates for Savonarola can see in this offer only an attempt to withdraw him from Florence, thus effectively closing his sermons. According to these writers Savonarola took the matter in the sense of bartering, and as such, repudiated it. They cite in support of their opinion his blunt answer to the Pope's messenger: "Come to my next sermon and you will receive my answer to Rome;" and his public declaration, often repeated in other discourses, "I desire neither

special provisions having been made to accommodate the multitude eager to hear the restored preacher. Guarded by his friends, Savonarola proceeded to the church. Even then his life was in danger, for the *Arrabbiati* were determined to assassinate him. Mounting the pulpit, he yielded to the inspiration of the scene. Clearly, solemnly, tenderly, he proclaimed his Catholic Faith, and his unswerving loyalty to the Holy See, with whose permission he had resumed his preaching. The discourse was a splendid effort, a demonstration, if one were needed, that Savonarola was an orator of marvellous power.

He defended his attitude towards the summons to Rome; he defied his enemies; he lashed the vices and crimes that were stalking abroad in the land; he denounced superstition; he pointed out the dangers of mere ceremonies and external observances when faith was dead; he pleaded for a renewal of the spiritual life, for perseverance by those who had already entered on the penitential way. Thus he continued during Lent. Some of his utterances as to coming plagues and the ruin and desecration of churches were afterwards fulfilled. His courage was admirable, but his enemies were increasing. Too many had felt the sting of his lash; too many saw themselves in a hideous reflection as he held before Florence the mirror of the Christian life. Moreover, his strained relations with the Pope stripped him somewhat of the old-time power, while his distinctions as to a collision between conscience and a superior's command, bred among his hearers suspicions and evil thoughts.

hats nor mitres; I desire only what the saints received; I desire only death, yea, a red hat, a hat crimson with my blood." Possibly a simple solution and a more truthful one may be found in Savonarola's humility.

XV

MISSIONARY AND LITERARY LABOURS—
RENEWED CONTENTION WITH THE POPE
(1496)

✠

A FTER EASTER, 1496, Savonarola proceeded to Prato, in which city the Dominican Convent, as we have already mentioned, had been placed under his jurisdiction. His stay in Prato was short, but his preaching bore abundant fruit. In May he resumed his labours in Florence. He preached chiefly on Sundays, and published two volumes, Israel; —one on the simplicity of the Christian life, in which he presented Catholic truths in a style so easy that all who ran might read; the other volume contained an exposition of the seventy-ninth Psalm: "Give ear, O Thou that rulest Thou that leadest Joseph like a sheep." From May until late in August he continued at intervals his impassioned sermons in which warnings and menaces of future retribution were repeated often. He was entirely divested of all human fear. On August 20th, he preached in the Hall of the Grand Council; and there, before the Signoria, the other officials, and the leading men of Florence, he defended himself against the slurs of the enemies who had impugned his motives, and who, by dishonestly charging him with undue interference in public affairs, had slandered him.

At this time, the Republic being in sore straits,[1] the powerful influence of Savonarola was eagerly sought by the authorities; and, despite the ingratitude which he had already experienced, he generously devoted his time to the strengthening of the government among the people. With rare prudence he avoided giving the Pontiff any further occasion for irritation. In fact, during two months and more he abstained from preaching; it was late in October when he again ascended the pulpit. Great misery prevailed in the city, and the unfortunate people turned to the prior in the hope of some relief. He encouraged them, comforted them, and to win special favour from Heaven, he organised a grand procession in honour of the Blessed Virgin. The image of the Madonna dell' Impruneta having been brought into the city, the Florentines, who specially venerated our Lady under this title, manifested an extraordinary devotion.[2]

While the procession was in progress, news came that much needed supplies were at hand. Considering this as a sign of heavenly favour, the fickle multitude again hailed Savonarola as their deliverer. On All Saints' and All Souls' Savonarola again preached. Five days later the Pope issued another Brief, in which he took a stand entirely different from that of his previous order, regarding the union of the Tuscan and the Lombard provinces of the Order. By this latest letter he commanded the Florentine and Tuscan Dominicans to unite in one province with those of the Roman congregation, under a vicar who would be immediately subject to the Master General of the Order. In answer to this Brief, Savonarola published an apology, in which he contended that the Pope had been misinformed and that to

1   The war against Pisa was still under way; famine had stricken parts of Tuscany; pestilence also prevailed.

2   Near the celebrated Certosa, about twelve miles from Florence, lies the village of Impruneta. There, in the church of the *Madonna dell' Impruneta*, is enshrined a miraculous painting of our Lady, attributed to St. Luke. Among the Tuscans, this shrine is still highly venerated.

carry out his command would be to the detriment of religion. Frankly, we can offer no excuse for Savonarola's action in this crisis. Forgetting his previous declaration that he would obey, though the ruin of the world followed, he refused to carry out the injunctions of Alexander. And yet the command of the Pope was not only within his right, waiving all question of motive,[3] but it was his further right, had he so desired, to suppress the province over which Savonarola ruled, or the entire Order of which he was a member.

Had the prior of San Marco's obeyed, yielding up his authority and becoming subject to the new jurisdiction, he might have been transferred from Florence (where he believed his presence necessary), he might have been silenced, he might have been persecuted, but worse could not have befallen him than awaited him in ungrateful Florence, nor would he have lost the victory which is ever promised to the obedient man. The twenty-sixth of November found him again in the pulpit ; he continued to preach during Advent, giving a marked political character to his discourses, and sounding a note of defiance that meant "no retreat, no surrender." This alone would have placed him in a false position. A semblance of power he held; but the plots, forgeries, and slanders of his enemies, together with his own defiance of the Pope, were already paving the way for the end of his seeming triumph. When the year 1496 closed, his position was one of great peril.

He defended his attitude towards the summons to Rome; he defied his enemies; he lashed the vices and crimes that were stalking abroad in the land; he denounced superstition; he pointed out the dangers of mere ceremonies and external observances when faith was dead; he pleaded for a renewal of the spiritual life, for perseverance by those who had already entered on the penitential way. Thus he continued during Lent. Some of his utterances as to coming plagues and the ruin and

---

3   Villari sees in the changed policy of Alexander only the dominating influence of politics. Our comment is: what about Savonarola's variations?

desecration of churches were afterwards fulfilled. His courage was admirable, but his enemies were increasing. Too many had felt the sting of his lash; too many saw themselves in a hideous reflection as he held before Florence the mirror of the Christian life. Moreover, his strained relations with the Pope stripped him somewhat of the old-time power, while his distinctions as to a collision between conscience and a superior's command, bred among his hearers suspicions and evil thoughts.

XVI

PLOTS OF THE FRIAR'S ENEMIES—
BURNING OF THE VANITIES
(1497)

✠

A S THE LENT of 1497 drew near, the *Arrabbiati*, and especially the younger portion of them, many of whom had banded together and were known as the *Compagnacci*¹ determined to cast off the restraints which Savonarola's reform had put upon their amusements. It is apparent that the prior had not sufficiently consulted the reasonable weaknesses of human nature, and so his advice and rules concerning entertainment bore the stamp of excessive severity. Against these, the "bad fellows" not only rebelled, but they also resolved to go to the other extreme, reviving the shameful practices that had been in vogue during the Medicean rule. Savonarola was on the alert, and was ably seconded by his devoted disciple, Father Dominic, who preached daily, while the prior occupied himself in the composition and publication of various pamphlets, and in the final draft of his book on "The Triumph of the Cross." The *Arrabbiati* and the *Compagnacci* were defeated, and by a peculiar device as we shall now see.

¹   The bad fellows.

Once more Savonarola won the children, who paraded the city for several days before the Carnival, making a novel collection from the people already disposed, through the sermons of Savonarola and Father Dominic, to surrender vain and sinful objects. A large quantity of miscellaneous articles was secured. Preparations had been made in the Piazza, where an enormous pyramid had been erected, sixty feet in height, divided, as Burlamacchi relates, into fifteen tiers, or as another contemporary reports, into seven, symbolising the seven deadly sins. The interior of the pyramid was filled with inflammable material. We follow Burlamacchi as to the disposition of the articles which had been collected by the children:

> On the first step were laid the foreign tapestries on which obscene figures had been wrought; on the second were pictures of Florentine damsels, and other representations; on the next were cards, dice, gambling implements; on the fourth were musical instruments; then came women's adornments—false hair, perfumes, lotions, powders, etc.; after these were placed copies of the profane poets and some of the modern writers, Boccaccio and others finally a great quantity of Carnival finery—masks, costumes, etc. Surmounting all was a figure of King Carnival.

The news had spread rapidly, and the curiosity and excitement of the Florentines were aroused to a high pitch. In great numbers the people assembled, after the religious exercises of the morning—Mass, Communion by all the children, and a grand procession, during which a generous collection of money was made for the "Good Men of St. Martin." Suddenly, at four points the pile was fired, and, while the air was filled with the sweet song of the children, the huge pyramid was consumed.

Probably no event in Savonarola's career has excited more bitter condemnation than this "burning of the vanities."[2] Exaggeration, both by friends and opponents, has so exalted the value

2   As early as 1425 the great Franciscan missionary, St. Bernardine of Siena, made a similar "bonfire" of vanities in Perugia.

and the nature of the stuff destroyed, that it is difficult to arrive at a certain conclusion. The alleged offer, by a Venetian who was present, of twenty thousand crowns for the articles on the pyramid, had something to do with the erroneous notions prevailing as to the quality of the "vanities." In consequence, Savonarola has been denounced as a barbarous hater of the arts, an iconoclast, a gloomy fanatic opposed to all innocent enjoyment. The old complaint of Judas—why were not these things sold and their price given to the poor?—has also been brought against the friar.

These objections have been satisfactorily met. At a time famous for its scholars, many of whom witnessed this burning under the direction of a man who was himself a poet, whose convent was a sanctuary of art, whose most devoted friends were the painters and sculptors of the day, it is not likely that any really precious article was destroyed. In burning obscenely illustrated volumes, some rare editions may have been destroyed; among the paintings, there may have been some inferior works of eminent artists; but the great bulk of the "vanities" were composed of masks, wigs, beards, toilet articles, etc., cheap stuff whose sale would have brought little for the poor, of whom Savonarola had always taken good care.

In proof of his positive statement that art had not suffered by this burning, and as a testimony to the noble and generous spirit of the scholarly prior of San Marco's, Villari refers to the purchase by Savonarola of the Medicean library, under circumstances of peculiar honour to the friar and his brethren, who stripped themselves of many of their possessions, and burdened themselves with debt to keep intact this splendid collection, and to preserve it for Florence. At the same time Savonarola was, in this special instance, the financial mainstay of the Government, which was passing through a period of great stringency.

"Here then," writes Villari, "is historical proof that the supposed enemy of the ancients, the barbarous destroyer of manuscripts and works of art, not only devoted the last remnant of

his Convent's property, but likewise burdened the community
with a very heavy debt, in order to preserve to art and science
the marvellous collection of Greek and Latin codices, and the
unrivalled treasure of miniatures still contained in the Lauren-
tian Library."

Anticipating, as we may, we shall hereafter to the second
burning which took place in 1498. It differed but little from the
burning of the previous year, though the preliminary procession
and the begging of alms for the "Good men of St. Martin" were
interrupted by the *Compagnacci* who insulted *Piagnoni*, and in
various offensive and injurious ways proved their right to their
ugly title. Speaking of this burning, Villari quotes Nardi, a lover
of antiquity, a scholar and historian who declares that "many dishonest, indecent, and vain things were burned;" and Somenzi,
an enemy of Savonarola, who wrote that the pile consisted "of
a great quantity of lustful things, mirrors, women's false hair,
masks, paintings, quantities of perfumes, and every species of
lustful things." "Is it likely," asks Villari, "that if really valuable
objects of art had been included in the collection, the learned
Nardi, and Somenzi, the bitter enemy of Savonarola, would have
failed to mention the fact?"

Cathedral of Santa Maria del Fiore: The Duomo of Florence.

XVII

✠

THE LENT OF 1497 practically closed the effective preaching of Savonarola. Though his difficulty with Alexander VI was approaching an acute stage, and though he continued to denounce abuses, he made it clear to all that he questioned no dogma of the Church, that he not only recognized the supreme spiritual dominion of Rome, but also that he was a loyal upholder of the temporal sovereignty of the Holy See. Expecting, as it would seem, the excommunication which later fell on him, he showed a spirit of strange courage or defiance. Again he referred to his violent death, as he foresaw it, and cheerfully offered his life as a sacrifice. Political questions in which Alexander was deeply concerned, still held a place in the dispute. To the Florentines he made overtures regarding Pisa which were not accepted. For this he rebuked their ambassador, affirming that the Republic resisted him because of their faith in the friar who, as he declared, had insulted the Holy See. In Rome intrigues were incessant among Piero de' Medici's adherents, one of whose most devoted followers was the friar Mariano, who had been humiliated in Florence, and who had transferred his residence to Rome, where he kept up his spiteful opposition to Savonarola.

In Florence plots were hatched, and desperate efforts were made to arouse a sentiment in favour of the return of Piero, who was planning to enter the city by force. He failed ignominiously. Savonarola had predicted his humiliating retreat. The *Compagnacci* were foremost among those who sought the downfall of the prior as a preliminary to the downfall of the Republic. They had resolved on his assassination. They resorted to the most disgraceful and cowardly tactics to harass him. They profaned the Duomo in a shameful and filthy manner. His Ascension Day sermon they sacrilegiously interrupted; they tried to precipitate a riot, and while he fearlessly stood in the pulpit, vainly endeavouring to make himself heard above the noise, the wretches attempted to kill him. It seems almost incredible that Alexander could have sanctioned such an outrage, yet the charge is made against him, without the offer of any proof except that of another unproven charge that he had been withholding a brief of excommunication, awaiting the result of Piero's expedition, and of the plot against Savonarola.

Nine days after the Ascension sermon the excommunication was launched.[1] The document, however, had not reached Florence on the 22nd,[2] nor was it then known, except by way of foreboding, when Savonarola addressed to Alexander a conciliatory letter, appealing against his enemies, and referring to his forthcoming work, "The Triumph of the Cross," for a justification of his teachings. On two points, however, there can be no dispute. Alexander charged Savonarola with disobedience in the affair of the Tuscan Congregation already related ; but he did not charge him with heresy. Repeating the former style of reference to "a

1   Excommunication is a punishment inflicted by the Church when, in the exercise of her supreme power, she severs an individual from her Communion. See *A Catholic Dictionary* for a fuller explanation.

2   We find no proof for Villari's statement that Alexander, on receiving this letter, expressed regret for the publication of his Brief at that time. For text of Savonarola's letter, see Appendix I.

certain friar, Jerome, said to be Vicar," etc., Alexander declared that from reports the said friar was suspected of heresy. This, however, availed little. A terrible blow fell on Savonarola when, by mid-June, the papal edict had been solemnly promulgated, to be followed by all the attending misfortunes awaiting one with whom no Christian could hold communion.

The effect of such a measure cannot be estimated by those unfamiliar with the dreadful consequences involved in the infliction of these penalties of last ecclesiastical resort. Savonarola bowed before the storm; kept within his cloister; but in a declaration to "all Christians in the love of God," he defended himself, and denied the justice and the validity of the excommunication. In the meantime the *Compagnacci* had asserted themselves, and Florence, true to the lowest instinct of ungrateful humanity, resumed its course of evil as in the worst days from which Savonarola had rescued it. Within a month the city was the scene of every manner of disorder, —the vile rabble even going the length of stoning the Convent of San Marco's. For this offence they were not punished by the Signoria then in power, which contained a majority opposed to Savonarola. During July and August, however, a new election brought the prior's friends to the front, and then began a series of most earnest efforts on the part of the Signoria, of the Florentine ambassador at Rome, and of influential followers of Savonarola, to secure the repeal of the Brief of excommunication.[3]

The brethren of San Marco's, and hundreds of the leading citizens of Florence, signed petitions begging absolution for

---

3   A grave and scandalous incident "with Father Marchese mentions occurred about this time. It was intimated very clearly to Savonarola that the payment of a debt of five thousand crowns to the creditor of a certain cardinal would be followed by the raising of the ban. Needless to say, Savonarola indignantly spurned the offer. In the midst of these trying events Alexander's son, the Duke of Gandia, had been assassinated. Savonarola wrote to the Pope offering him consolation, and urging him to persevere in the newness of life on which, through grief for his son's untimely death, he was said to have entered. Alas! It was only a temporary change, followed by renewed anger against the prior for "insulting his fatherly sorrow." The reader is reminded that Alexander had been married before entering the priesthood.

Savonarola, and bearing testimony to the holiness of his life and doctrine. It was all in vain. His enemies were powerful, and their activity was unceasing. As July advanced, the plague, which had broken out, spread rapidly, though it spent its force before the end of August. While it continued, Savonarola, though unable to minister spiritually to the afflicted because of his excommunication, was unsparing in his efforts to succour them through material aid, counsel, encouragement, letters of guidance, and pamphlets of practical instruction, and by the example of his own unfaltering fortitude.

XVIII

✠

THE CESSATION OF the pestilence, and the consequent resumption of the usual course of affairs, afforded the government an opportunity to take up the case of those who had been suspected of complicity in the recent attempt of Piero de' Medici to regain his hold on the Republic. As the result of an exciting trial, five distinguished citizens were sentenced to death.

In the matter of this conspiracy and trial Savonarola has been grievously maligned. As Villari pointedly remarks, "Neither in the histories, memoirs, correspondence, or biographies, of the period do we find a single word to indicate whether Savonarola was favourable or unfavourable to the accused." His own declaration is evidence that he had deprecated the death penalty for the leader, and that he had recommended another to the consideration of friends. Nevertheless, he has been represented as denying to the condemned the right of appeal, as if the administration of law and judicial decisions rested with him.[1]

In this charge there are two errors. The guilt of the conspirators having been conclusively proved, after an exhaustive and protracted trial with which Savonarola had no connection whatever, he could not have saved them, on an appeal, even had he made the attempt; because patriotic passion was running too high to suffer any check, even from the friar. The further assertion that the law of appeal denied to the condemned was of his making is one of those half-truths which are often worse than whole lies. Savonarola, as we have narrated in its proper place, had striven to secure the establishment of a court of appeal, not the final reference of judicial cases to a mob.

The autumn of 1497 was passing, and Savonarola, silent and withdrawn from the public eye, laboured with extraordinary diligence in the composition and publication of various spiritual works, letters, tracts, pamphlets, for religious and for the laity. Toiling tirelessly, he published a small library of these treatises in an incredibly short time. He also finished his great book, *The Triumph of the Cross*,[2] which, though based on St. Thomas Aquinas' *Summa Contra Gentiles*, is one of the earliest attempts made by a theologian to treat religion from the view-point of reason. In this work he proved that he was a deep thinker; he manifested great courage in disregarding the beaten paths of his day, while his fidelity to the Angelic Doctor, his vast learning, and his undoubted orthodoxy, make the volume his Catholic monument.[3] Beginning with the existence of God and the necessity

1   Savonarola is numbered among the legislators of Florence; but he never interfered in the administration of affairs, beyond the share he had in establishing the government after the expulsion of Piero de' Medici.

2   This work has been translated into English by a Protestant writer, O'Dell T. Hill, who showed not only bad taste and bigotry, but also took an unwarranted liberty with the author's teaching, by omitting his strong, clear, Catholic assertion of the Pope's rights and powers. [Editor's note: Subsequent translations of better quality are available and have been done by the English Dominican Fr. John Procter O.P. and by our society. See The Savonarola Project for more information]

3   Savonarola's devotion to St. Thomas Aquinas is also manifested in his work treating the Government of Florence. In this, he adheres to the principles of his

of religion, he proceeds to the Christian revelation, passes to its doctrines and sacraments, and concludes with a refutation of opposing and contradictory creeds.

Had men seriously doubted the great preacher's loyal Catholicity, this volume (a pioneer of a new school of spiritual literature), in matter most solid and excellent, in style most original, would have been an explicit and a satisfactory answer. Neither heretic nor schismatic was Savonarola; no more devoted son of the Roman See ever laboured for God and souls, despite his unhappy collision with Alexander the Sixth.

All other efforts at reconciliation having failed, the Republic having exhausted all its influence, Pico della Mirandola published an apology for the friar, in which he showed much learning; but he failed to touch the main point, —the duty of obedience to a command, even though the most unworthy motives animate the superior. History, as usually written, may not absolve Alexander from the gratuitous charge of harbouring sentiments of personal animosity against Savonarola, is it likely to free him from another charge of having used the spiritual weapons of the Church in an affair from which politics could not be separated. The domain of motive and conscience is here entered without sufficient external light to guide the inquirer; judgement, therefore, should at least be suspended. Is it not also evident that an impartial judgement must deplore the error of Savonarola, who allowed himself to take a false stand through excessive zeal?

In celebrating Mass on Christmas, 1497, and in preaching on Septuagesima Sunday, 1498, while under the ban of excommunication, Savonarola probably acted on the dictates of a conscience which may have grown certain in the conviction that his excommunication was unjust and invalid. Nevertheless, we deplore this step as a "blunder worse than a crime." It proved to be "the beginning of the end."

master, as taught in the De Regimine Principum. Symonds considers this treatise of Savonarola to be the "most thorough-going analysis of despotic criminality."

He pleaded his cause ably, but the tide had set strongly against him, and was flowing fast. Three times subsequently he spoke before the end of the Carnival, which he closed with the second burning of the vanities. It was on this day that, holding aloft the Blessed Sacrament, he solemnly called God to destroy him if he had ever spoken falsely to the people.[4] The report of these happenings was carried to Rome, where powerful enemies were engaged in a final effort to overcome the friar. Alexander's anger was natural, for seldom had a Pope been defied in such a manner. He was also incensed against the Republic for its advocacy and support of the daring friar. The contention was further inflamed by Father Mariano, who preached a violent and opprobrious sermon against Savonarola, though his evident malice and gross buffoonery won for him only increased contempt and reprobation. From this, however, he derived fresh zeal in his malignant pursuit of a man who had never injured him. On February 26th Alexander wrote to the Signoria, and commanded them to stop Savonarola's preaching, and either to send him to Rome, or to imprison him in Florence. The Brief closed with the threat of an interdict on the city. But the Signoria were not moved. The canons of the cathedral, however, had also received a command to prevent the friar from speaking in the Duomo. Accordingly he withdrew to San Marco's, where his audience was so great that a special day was set for the exclusive attendance of women.

The election for March and April returned a majority of the Signoria opposed to Savonarola. It is puzzling, therefore, to find these men writing to Alexander on behalf of the prior. Villari inclines to the opinion that their purpose was still further to vex and irritate the Pope. Savonarola continued his sermons on the reformation of the Church, and on the need of a Council. Reading these discourses after four hundred years, it must be admitted that Alexander showed considerable patience. Some

---

4   A celebrated writer, referring to this extraordinary prayer, introduces the gentle fall of a sunbeam on the upturned, radiant face of the friar, which the people took as a heavenly sign. His contemporaries mention no such occurrence.

writers call this patience, cunning and duplicity. But even were it so, the condition of affairs had now come to such a pass that the end was only a question of a short time. Repeatedly the Pope warned the Florentine government that he would brook no further delay. He had grown tired of words; he demanded deeds. And not until these deeds were accomplished would he consider favourably the Republic's request regarding Pisa and the proposed taxation of church property. He denied that he had been misinformed, he admitted the good works; the correct teaching of Savonarola; but he also insisted on his submission and obedience. On receiving these he would absolve him, and allow him to resume his place in the pulpit. Otherwise he would at once interdict the city.[5]

During this time—the month of March—Piero de' Medici was active in Rome, securing cooperation for the decisive moment when he should again attempt to regain control in Florence. The other enemies of Savonarola were incessant in their plotting, while the Venetians and the Milanese, encouraged by Alexander, were seeking, if possible, to force the Florentines into their league. Politics dominated and confused the minds of the friends and foes of the friar. Many of his friends grew timid, especially when the threatened interdict was held over their heads. Commercial and financial considerations also had great weight, for an interdict meant the business ruin of a city while it continued in force. It was not, therefore, religion or loyalty to the Pope, but selfish, material interests that won to Alexander's side a majority of the government, now ready to sacrifice the friar who had done so much and so generously for the city which was about to abandon him. On March 15th Savonarola, as if urged to make a last appeal directly to the Pope, wrote to Alexander a

5   An interdict is an ecclesiastical censure by which persons are debarred from the use of certain sacraments, from all the divine offices, and from Christian burial. The infliction of such a penalty, like every war measure, involved the innocent as well as the guilty. The Church has rarely used this punishment, though history records instances of its exercise against cities, churches, and individuals. The reader will find a plain statement of the nature and effects of interdicts in *A Catholic Dictionary*.

letter full of affection and courage. Fearing, he said, that no hope could be entertained of a revocation of the decree of excommunication, he must therefore appeal to God, for Whom he was ready, longing, to lay down his life; and he closed by warning Alexander to consider his ways, and not to delay the affair of his salvation. On the 17th, he preached in San Marco's, and on the evening of the same day he received a communication from the Signoria requesting him to discontinue his sermons. He told the messengers that his answer would be given on the next day. On the 18th Savonarola delivered his farewell discourse, crowning in sorrow and humiliation (though still deeper depths were in waiting) an unexampled career of devotion to the best interests of Florence; a devotion manifested in his marvellous sermons during eight years, and in the numerous other good works with which he had blessed the Republic.

XIX

The Trial by Fire
(1498)

✠

SAVONAROLA'S EFFORTS TO secure the summoning of a Council for the reformation of the Church and for the deposition of Alexander VI must not be judged in the light of our day. The wounds inflicted by the great Schism of the West, the Church still bore in her body. The notions prevailing as to the power of a Council were exaggerated; peculiar also were the views held by more than one king. The monstrous evils which Savonarola clearly saw and bitterly felt seemed to him to justify his appeal to the Catholic sovereigns of England, Germany, France, Spain, and Hungary. Moreover, he relied on the cardinals, many of whom, notably the Cardinal of St. Peter in Chains, were strongly opposed to Alexander, and had seemed anxious to secure his deposition or resignation. The letters prepared for the monarchs were not Preliminary correspondence, however, had been arranged through friends in the different countries. These communications were sufficiently clear to outline the bold plan contemplated by Savonarola. Unfortunately the courier carrying the packet intended for the Florentine ambassador in France was seized by spies of the Duke of Milan, who, to win favour with

Alexander, at once sent to Rome the incriminating documents. Savonarola's doom was sealed. Alone he could not contend, with success, against the mighty power of his combined foes; he declined, nevertheless, to attempt escape, resolved to meet his fate in the same lofty spirit with which he had invited it.

The majority of those holding political power in Florence completely turned against him, and even the Franciscans, who in the history of their institute had ever been affectionately united with the Dominicans, contributed an antagonist to swell the growing number of the unhappy prior's enemies. On the rapidly increasing misfortunes of a brave and unselfish man, prematurely worn with fasting, labour, suffering, and care, a miserable culmination was put, before the tragic ending, by the precipitation of an abortive "trial by fire." Friar Francis di Puglia is the name of the man who has achieved an unenviable notoriety as a challenger of Savonarola to the wretched and barbarous device of the "Trial." After vilifying the prior in an unchristian manner, Francis had the audacity to summon him to the ordeal by fire, through which the Franciscan declared his readiness to prove the great Dominican a heretic and a false prophet. Savonarola had previously been annoyed by such challenges, but he had always ignored them, despising the barbarity as well as the unreasonableness of such "proofs." He treated the arrogant Franciscan in like manner.

Here the matter might have ended, in deserved contempt, had it not been for Father Dominic, who came forward and recognized the Franciscan as one who during the previous year had challenged him to a dispute, and then had run away. On behalf of Savonarola, Father Dominic took up the gauntlet which Father Francis had thrown down. Again he proved recreant. Pretending that he had no cause with Father Dominic and that with Savonarola only he could deal, he hastily took advantage of the way thus opened to him for escape. But Father Dominic pursued the case with great eagerness, despite the warning and reproval of Savonarola, who wished him to pay no further heed to the affair. The *Compagnacci* then became interested and used their influence with the Signoria to push the matter, so that the people might enjoy a spectacle.

This would have afforded a desirable opportunity for these dissolute young men to raise a tumult, in the confusion of which they would either seize Savonarola or kill him. A real "ordeal" was not desired by either the Signoria or the *Compagnacci*. The Franciscan seems to have understood that he would not be in danger, even if some of the Dominicans were burned. Nevertheless, he provided, like many patriots, a substitute. The arrangements, however, dragged slowly; it was the end of March before they were concluded. Alexander had heard of the contemplated ordeal, but he did not prohibit the exhibition. He had other cares. Despite his good judgement which condemned such a senseless encounter, despite the fact that he strenuously opposed the "ordeal." Savonarola felt that God would vindicate the brethren of San Marco's against whom much bitterness had been aroused. The government openly favoured the Franciscans. This injustice only excited the zeal of Savonarola's followers, among whom not only were several hundred friars found ready to volunteer to undergo the terrible trial, but many laymen and even women. Of this striking fact the Pope was made aware through a letter sent to him bearing exclusively on this extraordinary demonstration. Savonarola published a statement and defence against his accusers, for his slanderers hesitated at no untruth. Obligated to take action, he took it boldly. He declared that for every Friar Minor who would appear at the trial a Dominican champion would be ready. The 6th of April was the day assigned for the ordeal. On the 5th San Marco's Community received notice of a postponement to the 7th. The Dominicans who had been enthusiastic for the contest felt disappointed, but stood ready for the 7th. Despite the assurances given to them of immunity from danger, despite the grievous penalties which had been decreed against their opponents in case of failure, the Franciscans demanded further guarantees. These were granted

in the form of a resolution by the Signoria, which provided that
if Father Dominic perished in the flames, Savonarola would be
banished within three hours.

How absurd it all seems! How barbarous and un-Christian!
Yet these were times of a certain refinement, of much learning,
of great faith; but also, alas of great superstition, of shameful
depravity, of legal methods that remind us of savages; and men,
even of Savonarola's stature were, to an extent, under the spell!

It is not necessary to dwell in further detail on this farcical
ordeal. The Dominicans attended; the Franciscans appeared,
after much delay, and then, with various unworthy quibbles
and tricky subterfuges. The day passed; there was no spectacle. The disappointed throngs that had stood for hours, eager
to witness the barbarous ordeal, dispersed with anger in their
hearts against Savonarola, who had not faltered; but, mob-like,
with applause for his opponents, who had shirked the contest
in a cowardly fashion, every concession finding them still more
reluctant to meet the adversaries whom they had challenged to
the trial. Human nature, in Florence, as the world over, in the
waning days of the fifteenth century, as in the period of refined
and delicate civilization which the nineteenth claims as its own,
was proving its title to littleness, ingratitude, and cruelty.

Escorted by devoted adherents, who defended them with
drawn swords (and it was necessary), the Dominicans found
their return to San Marco's a difficult and perilous journey. The
Compagnacci were nimble in insult and outrage, and, of course,
the mob joined them. But the gallant followers of Marsuccio
Salviati (whose resolute threat, that he would cut down any
man who crossed the line of safety he had drawn around his
revered friars, was well understood), conducted to San Marco's
the Prior and his brethren, who had been subjected to so mor-
tifying a deception by the infamous plotters and their tools, the
misguided Minors. In a few days the *Compagnacci* and all the
other enemies of the now helpless and doomed victim were able
to celebrate a triumph which was the beginning of Florence's

downfall. "The death of the friar," said Pope Julius II., "preceded by a few years the death of the Republic."

Cloister of St. Antoninus at the Convent of San Marco.

XX

THE ATTACK ON SAN MARCO—ARREST OF THE FRIAR

✠

EVENTS NOW RUSHED to their conclusion. Many of the supporters of Savonarola were disappointed. They had hoped, and indeed believed, that he would enter the fire, and come out unscathed, to the confusion of his enemies. The *Arrabbiati* and *Compagnacci*, seeing the hesitation of those in power, who still clung to the fallen prior, re-doubled their vicious efforts, determined to strike the first blow, to shed the first blood. Alone with God, Savonarola passed the evening of the "ordeal." His great heart must have known the depths of agony, as wave after wave of doubt, of regret, of disappointment, of humiliation, of cruellest ingratitude, swept over his soul, engulfing him as in a sea of woe. The next day was Palm Sunday. He made a short address in the morning. Seeming to realise the catastrophe that was impending, he again proclaimed his readiness to die, to seal with his blood the purity, the truth, the honour, the glory, of the doctrine he had preached, and the life he had lived.

His enraged and already triumphant enemies took him at his word. The *Compagnacci* precipitated a quarrel with some of the *Piagnoni*. They prevented a Dominican from speaking in the cathedral, and this outrage, they followed by brutally kill-

ing two unoffending men whom they met on the street. Then
the murderous ruffians rushed to San Marco's, and as the friars
were chanting Vespers, on the inoffensive worshippers, men,
women, and children, the cowardly and sacrilegious wretches
rained a storm of stones. In terror the people fled, bruised,
wounded, many of them trampled underfoot in their mad effort
to gain the street. Quickly were the doors of church and convent
barred, while a small band, thirty in number, of determined men
remained within, resolved to defend the house of God and the
brethren. Unknown to Savonarola, a few shields and muskets
had been stored in the convent cellar by some of his friends, in
view of an anticipated attack. On seeing the warlike preparations
for defence, he forbade all violence, and declared that he would
surrender himself to avoid bloodshed. His wishes were disregarded by some of the brethren as well as by the laymen; neither
would they permit him to depart. For several hours the contest
was waged with obstinacy on the part of the besiegers, with great
courage on the part of the handful of defenders. In cloister, in
corridors, in choir, and in church, the fight was sustained. From
the altar and the pulpit gunshots rang out, while crucifix and
candlestick were seized as ready weapons by the friars whom
Savonarola could not restrain, resolved as they were to protect
their home, and to sell their lives as brave men.

To the shame of the government, no help was sent to the
beleaguered convent. Rather the rioters were encouraged, while
their partisans flocked to their aid. The noble Valori, Savonarola's
ever-loyal friend, was cut down in the street while on his way to
gather reinforcements for the convent, and a few minutes later
his wife was foully assassinated by the infuriated rabble, who
then sacked his house. Even these murders did not move the
Signoria to punish the guilty. On the contrary, they sent several
orders to the convent, demanding that the innocent defenders
lay down their arms, and finally that Savonarola and Fathers
Dominic and Sylvester should be arrested.

The parting of the prior from his brethren, from the living, the dead, and the dying defenders of his beloved San Marco's, which he was to leave, alas! forever, was a scene of tenderness, resignation, courage, religion. Late at night, bound, and surrounded by a howling mob that heaped insults, imprecations, and blows on him, the fallen leader was dragged to prison. In an adjoining cell, Father Dominic was placed. On the following day Father Sylvester was arrested, and brought to share their confinement.

Misleading reports were sent by the Signoria to various courts, and to Alexander a petition was also addressed craving absolution for the bloody and sacrilegious work that had been done, asking permission to try the ecclesiastics; and like cunning but overreaching politicians, they added their former request that they might be authorised to tax churches. To these "worthy sons of Holy Church," to the sacrilegious cowards and murderers, greeting came with permission to try, which meant in that cruel age to torture, the poor prisoners. Alexander added that the condemned should be sent to him for punishment. Of course judgement had already been passed; their condemnation was assumed and assured. The Pope granted nothing as to the church taxes. At the same time tidings came of the death of Charles VIII. The miserable ending of the French monarch on the very day of the ordeal by fire, removed Savonarola's last earthly hope.

Drawing of the Convent of San Marco. Unedited image provided by Sailko according to the Creative Commons Attribution-Share Alike 3.0 Unported license: https://commons.wikimedia. org/wiki/File:Pianta_del_buonsignori,_dettaglio_097_san_marco_padri.jpg

XXI

Trial and Torture

✠

THE TRIAL OF Savonarola and his companions was a
mockery, an outrage on justice, whose merest forms
were preserved to cover and, if possible, to legalise a
premeditated judicial murder.

The papers stolen from the sacked convent gave no evidence
against the prior, nor could any incriminating testimony be
secured through the numerous arrests that followed the incarceration of the friars. The dastardly attempt of the captain of the
Compagnacci to rouse the people against Savonarola, by convey-
ing through the streets some of the weapons that had figured
in the storming of San Marco's, met with considerable success.
The discredited and imprisoned champion of their liberty was
held up to them as the despoiler of their freedom, as a violent
despot; and the stupid, ungrateful multitude believed the cruel
lie, and loudly clamoured for the death of the man who had
spent himself for them.

Florentine customs, intended to safeguard accused persons,
were ruthlessly set aside, while the laws that might have served
as a barrier against the conspirators were as recklessly trampled

underfoot. On the 14th of April, though Savonarola's torture began on the 9th, when he was first brought to the Council Hall, a new, irregular, illegal court was organized, composed of Savonarola's sworn enemies, at their head the infamous leader of the *Compagnacci*. The determination to convict was evident, no matter what the cost in fraud, outrage, perjury, or even torture.

We shall not linger over the agonising details; a summary of the proceedings will be sufficient. Broken with illness and labour, his originally delicate constitution having yielded to the austerities and toils which he had imposed on himself, Savonarola was led before his judges. He had already been questioned in an informal way. Again, according to the brutal code of the time, the torture was applied. Fiendish Indians, dancing in savage joy around their scalped victim, deserve our applause when contrasted with the civilised legislators of those days, who disgraced Christianity and humanity by their ingenious cruelty in dealing with accused persons.

Insulted, outraged, the prisoner, well-nigh exhausted by the terrible experience of the previous few days, was bound to the rope and pulley, and, having been lifted and suddenly dropped, his poor body was stretched till the bones and muscles were racked.[1] While in this condition he was questioned. The charges were under the three heads of faith, prophecies, and politics. The inhumanity of the examination by torture seems almost incredible yet these men were Christians, and their victim was a holy priest who had conferred most precious benefits upon them and their people. Savonarola's answers were in part clear, and again they were unsatisfactory;[2] in fact, he raved, amid his agonising cries to God that his soul might be delivered. Released from his bonds, he was ordered to write his declaration. He complied. The

---

1   This method of torture often rendered the victim delirious.

2   "Torment to lye sometimes will drive / Even the most innocent alive."
—*Ex Minis Publicanis*.

paper, however, was destroyed. It did not suit the evil purpose of his persecutors because it told only the truth.[3]

Relegated to his lonely cell, he was left to endure the sufferings of a wrenched and lacerated frame, as well as the sorrow that must have filled his soul on realising how abandoned and betrayed he was. With true religious spirit he prayed for his cruel enemies. In the meantime a wretch named Ceccone, who had received much kindness from Savonarola, which he repaid by acting as a spy for the Duke of Milan, offered his services (though the law debarred him, as secretary for the judges), guaranteeing that he would produce a deposition that would be effective. This traitor and perjurer was engaged.

In a few days the trial was resumed. For eleven days it continued, during which time we cannot state how often Savonarola was put to the torture but, as one eye-witness declared, he received on a certain day fourteen turns of the pulley. Hot coals were applied to the soles of his feet; and yet the infamous judges declared that he freely confessed, and was not under restraint of any kind. On only one count did he waver in his examination. His judges pressed the point as to prophecies, with great vehemence; but beyond a certain vagueness, a want of absolute conviction on his part, they could secure no evidence. On politics he was firm even in his delirium; on religion nothing could shake him at any time. He was no longer asked or allowed to write. Ceccone made all the notes as the examination proceeded; and subsequently he made a draft that was a tissue of forgeries, to which he secured the name of Savonarola, having first deceived him by reading the correct report, and then passing to him the one falsified, which he was directed to sign. Assuredly a diabolical plot!

Nevertheless, even this mutilated document did not contain sufficient to justify his death; rather did it establish his innocence. The traitorous secretary had signally failed in his endeavour.

3   See our extract from Napier, 134, 135.

Three days later the baffled conspirators put the prior to a second trial, again changing and distorting the depositions. This examination lasted four days, but its results were even more disappointing to his judges than were those of the first trial. Though the populace was perplexed, many saw clearly through the dishonest and illegal work of the Signoria, and of its corrupt judicial tools.

On April the 26th Father Dominic and Father Sylvester were summoned before the court. The former, ever loyal, ever heroic, if imprudent or impulsive at times, was the first to be subjected to the torture. Pulley and rack and iron boot were all used, but his splendid courage never failed. He even showed himself staunch against the villainous attempts made to weaken him through the false statements of his torturers that Savonarola had acknowledged himself an impostor and a false prophet. He wrote his deposition, and it also was distorted. Again and again they racked his poor body, but his undaunted spirit they could not break. Noble soul, worthy of a noble leader!

Father Sylvester failed under the torture. A weak man, who had not deserved the consideration shown to him by Savonarola, he yielded under the agony of the rack, and not only betrayed the names of the laymen who were friends of San Marco's, but even aspersed the character of the prior. Other friars and laymen were tortured, but nothing substantial resulted from the examinations that could incriminate Savonarola. On the contrary, despite the forgeries of Ceccone, the prior's innocence was more clearly established as a consequence of these trials. During these days of sorrow he languished in his cell, all communication with his brethren or with counsellors having been interdicted according to another delicate requirement of that refined period. While the helpless prior was suffering the agony of examination, the friars of San Marco, with few exceptions, also turned against him. Their petition to the Pope is a document that strangely contradicts their former life and conversation. They might have justly sought absolution, but it was not necessary for them to slander their prior; thus, offering another lesson of "ingratitude more strong than traitors' arms."

In the meantime the Pope and the Signoria were engaged in correspondence, the former demanding the surrender to him of Savonarola, the latter claiming the right of a sovereign state to execute condemned citizens, and adding, hypocritically, the specious pretext that, for example's sake, for the welfare of religion, the malefactor should be punished in the place where his notorious crimes had been committed. The unfortunate victim was held by the Florentines as a sort of price, in the hope of extorting from Alexander the ecclesiastical tax privilege they had so often requested, and for which Savonarola himself had so generously striven.[4] This must have been as the iron in his soul, but he spoke no word of impatience or resentment.

4   Subsequently the Pope granted, but only for three years, the ecclesiastical taxes in favour of the Government.

XXII

SOLITARY CONFINEMENT

✠

F ROM APRIL 25TH till May 19th Savonarola had been kept
in solitary confinement. In this interval much had been
accomplished. A new Signoria had been elected, even
more determined in its malignity than the retiring board. Papal
commissioners were despatched to Florence to preside at the
closing scenes, for by this time (May 11th) the death of the victims was considered as assured beyond any chance of mishap.

On May 19th the two Papal commissioners, Father Joachim
Turriano, Master General of the Dominicans, and Dr. Francis Romolino, a Spanish bishop, afterwards cardinal, arrived
in Florence. A Dominican prelate named Paganotti, Bishop of
Vasona, and apparently an auxiliary of the Archbishop of Florence, was designated by Alexander to degrade the friars, and
then to hand them over to the secular power.

"The very dregs of the people," as Villari writes, "flocked
around the commissioners as they entered the city, shouting
'Death to the friar!'" Bishop Romolino, in a spirit at least unbe-
coming to his office if not to his episcopal character, answered,
"Surely he will die." We may therefore credit the statements of

Burlamacchi, that letters had been received in Florence declaring that these commissioners had been instructed to put Savonarola to death even were he another John the Baptist and that Romolino, later in the day, brutally declared, "We shall have a great bonfire, for I have the sentence already prepared." Never in human affairs was there a viler prostitution of justice, never was there a more infamous outrage in the name of law! And shall we add in the name of religion?

Here let us return to the lonely prisoner in the tower, and to his two companions. During the time of their incarceration the three friars had been kept in close and solitary confinement. The legislation and jurisprudence of those days, as applied in courts and prisons, might well have been devised, as was said of the English penal laws against Ireland, by the arch enemy of men and in the infernal regions. Suspicion and superstition were in the air, nor was their influence upon laymen only. Father Dominic's red cope, his habit, his crucifix, were objected to on the day of the ordeal because of probable enchantment, a subtle force that his religious opponents also claimed might assert itself because of his standing near the Dominicans. And so, cope and habit and crucifix having been put away, the friar himself was ordered to stand apart. It was this narrow, unchristian spirit, bred of the lingering barbarism and paganism that prevailed among the Florentine authorities in their treatment of the noble prisoner and his companions.

Fortunately the torture had not entirely disabled his right hand—a hand that had never been lifted except in zealous warning or fatherly blessing; and so he spent the waiting hours in writing beautiful commentaries on the Thirtieth and Fiftieth Psalms: "In Thee, O Lord, have I hoped," and "Have mercy on me, O God, according to Thy great mercy." No complaint, no word of impatience, no countercharge, no defence, no expression that outraged innocence might, not unreasonably, have put forth, found its way into these writings. Only the soundest Catholic doctrine, the truest principles of the spiritual life, can be found in these tracts, the last legacy of the silenced preacher, who could now speak only with his eloquent pen. In the commentaries on the Fiftieth Psalm some have pretended to find the Protestant doctrine of justification by faith alone without good works. We shall dispose of this libel in another place. These treatises were rapidly disseminated, and were justly regarded with peculiar veneration.

Another instance of Savonarola's zeal and generous spirit we find in the service rendered to his jailer. This poor man, seeing with eyes unprejudiced, and from a heart in which no lurking hatred had left its poison, felt the goodness, the holiness, of the prisoner whose keeper he was. As a memorial that he would cherish, he begged Savonarola to write something for him. Without paper, having only the cover of a book, the prior wrote on this, in his wonderfully fine hand, a rule for virtuous living, in which he summed up, as a conclusion, the essentials of sacramental grace and good works. Thus, in these hours of pain and solitude, he dwelt with God, and thought only of his coming death as a release from earthly sorrow, and as an entrance to heavenly joys. Father Dominic and even Father Sylvester also manifested a truly religious and courageous spirit during these trying days.

Painting depicting the execution of fra Jerome Savonarola, Dominic of Pecia, and Sylvester of Florence in the Piazza della Signoria (circa 1500, unknown artist).

XXIII

EXECUTION OF SAVONAROLA

✠

O N MAY 20TH Savonarola was taken before the Papal commissioners for renewed torture and a third examination. The infamous Ceccone, assisted by other scribes worthy of his companionship in fraud and distortion, was present to record the prisoner's answers, and then to falsify them. This third so-called "trial" was even a more cruel and shameful mockery of law than were the preceding examinations. Now religion presided, in name but in fact, alas! The affair was a cowardly attempt by Florentine politicians to justify, in a legal fashion, a prearranged plan, a judgement already determined. Abominable questions were put to the tortured prior regarding his personal life. His acknowledged virtues had anticipated such questions in complete repudiation. As to the Council for which he had hoped, he spoke bravely. On no Italian potentates had he relied; for they were his enemies, and in the same category he placed the cardinals and other prelates.

Rendered delirious by the torture, he again raved, and spoke of the Cardinal of Naples as one cognisant of his plans; but on the return of reason, he retracted this statement. In the same noble spirit he abjured the denials that pulley and rope had before wrung from his wandering mind and helpless tongue. We contemplate with sentiments of pity the spectacle of those judges as they gazed, un-moved, on the prisoner now almost insane from pain, broken in body, and (as he held up his shattered arm) piteously crying out for mercy to Jesus Whom he thought he had denied. He had faltered during the previous trials, on the matter of the prophecies; he had denied that he possessed any supernatural endowment in the way of prophecy; but before his judges he now asserted what he felt to be the truth, and grievously deplored the weakness which had led him, as he too strongly put it, to deny God.

On the 21st and 22nd he was also tortured and examined. Promises alternated with threats, but he could not be shaken. His malignant judges attempted to frame a document embodying the falsified depositions of this third trial. Despite this fraudulent paper, without signature or witness, despite the ingenuity of Ceccone and of a band of citizens who sought, by surprise, an interview with the prior in his prison cell, hoping to entrap him in his words, the conspirators realised that they had no plea or justification in law that could be offered to the public. The barbarous work of six weeks of torture and of forgery had only one clear result—the innocence of the illustrious prisoner was made more manifest. On the third day of the examination by the Papal commissioners (the 22nd) the sentence, already resolved on, was formally decreed, —death by hanging, the bodies afterwards to be burned! On the same evening the three friars heard their fate. They were condemned to be executed early on the morrow.

Atrocious speed! But an evil deed, even as that of Judas, should be done quickly. The timid Sylvester received the tidings with great agitation; Dominic was full of joy; Savonarola manifested no feeling. He had already passed beyond the influence of earthly hope or fear. Only one word now would he speak, and that was to the member who came from the Company of the Temple, an organisation instituted for the solace of the dying. Through him the prior sought the favour of communicating with his two brethren. To this good man he also revealed, in a prophetic spirit, that woe would come upon the Church and Florence when a Pope named Clement should sit in Rome. And so it happened a generation later.[1]

Savonarola's request for an interview was reluctantly granted by the Signoria. In the hall of the Grand Council, the prior met his two spiritual sons. The hour went quickly by, nor on its sacredness may we intrude, though its beautiful lesson we shall note. The night wore away, and the lovely May morning in the glad Paschal time, the eve of the Ascension broke with a freshness and life that, to the weary victims, seemed but as the dawn of an everlasting day, the promise of their ascension from this vale of tears. All made a devout confession and were absolved. The prior was allowed to celebrate Mass. From his hands, his two companions received the Bread of Life. His profession of faith, in which they also joined, was a declaration of Catholic doctrine expressed in tender and touching words.

Then bare of foot and head, with hands bound, the three were led out. The scaffold had been erected; and for the bishop whose duty it was to degrade the ecclesiastics, for the Papal commissioners, and for the lay judges, places had been respectively arranged. The surrender of the scapular was the first demand made upon the three friars. As the distinctive mark of his habit, this deprivation was a severe trial to Savonarola. But he yielded bravely though with an aching heart. "I do not forsake thee, O holy scapular," he said, "gift of God, which I have ever kept without stain! How I longed to wear thee to the end, but now I am bereft of thee." The work of degrading the friars followed next.[2] "I separate thee," the bishop said, addressing Savonarola, "from the Church militant and," he added incautiously "from

---

1   [Editor's note: This prophecy would come to pass on May 6th, 1527, in the very same month and 29 years after the date of Savonarola's Martyrdom. This last prophecy is but another clear proof of his sanctity and his true status as a prophet of God.]

2   By degradation is understood the penalty inflicted on a cleric for certain very grievous offences, in consequence of which the person degraded is deprived of the privileges attaching to the clerical state, and as a layman may be handed over

the Church triumphant." —"From the Church militant, yes,"
replied Savonarola, "but from the Church triumphant, no; this
does not belong to you." The degraded friars, clad only in their
under tunics, were then passed to the Papal commissioners, who
pronounced condemnation against them for heresy and schism.
Finally they were delivered to the secular authorities, the bench
of judges, by whom the capital sentence was announced.

On hearing the result the mob shouted its insane approval, its
virtuous conviction that the men thus humiliated were indeed
guilty. "It is easy," a well-known writer has said, "to believe in
the damnable state of a man who stands stripped and degraded."
Then were seen the spirit of the leader and the docility of the
two disciples to the lessons of the last sad interview of the night
before. On their bowed heads the words of absolution had fallen,
and with reverence they had accepted the plenary indulgence
granted; but no word was spoken by them except in prayer.
Father Dominic's desire to be burned alive was no longer thought
of; Father Sylvester's determination to declare his innocence was
set aside. Previously he had recalled the untrue statements made
by him under torture. Both loyally and religiously went to their
death, as did their prior, silent, courageous, caring naught for
human justification, entirely resigned to the goodness of God.[3]

Savonarola was the last to be executed. Between his brethren his poor emaciated body swung suspended in ignominy
while the flames leaped high to make perfect the holocaust.
And while the fierce mob, full of hate, and gloating over the

to the civil power, even for the execution of capital punishment. See *A Catholic
Dictionary* for details

3   The shameful treatment accorded to the prisoners by the populace on the night
of their arrest was renewed on the morning of their execution. Some of the details
as given by Mirandola in his Latin life of Savonarola are unfit for presentation in
English. He mentions one man, guilty of a sacrilegious outrage, on whom, shortly
afterwards, the seeming, if not evident, judgement of God fell.
[Editor's note: This a reference to the disgusting man Giovanni Manetti who sup-
posedly to confirm a prophecy made by an astrologer that a hermaphrodite prophet
would emerge in Florence, molested the friar and subjected him to a degrading
physical examination of his genitals during his torture sessions, Manetti died
in anguish and despair, screaming "This hand, This hand!" This is recorded in
Burlamacchi.]

horrible spectacle, melted away; while the wicked judges and politicians went back to plot and to continue their work of persecution against the *Piagnoni*, some of whom even then were eagerly and devoutly seeking relics of their loved prophet and guide; the ashes were rudely gathered up, by command of the magistrates, and, having been carried to the river-bank, were wantonly scattered on the flowing waters of the Arno. Pitiable triumph of political vengeance!

Denied a tomb, the martyrs' memories were enshrined in the hearts of their faithful disciples.[4] For more than two hundred years, on each recurring 23rd of May, fragrant flowers were tenderly brought by loving hands, and reverently laid on a spot that to them was hallowed. Thus were treasured the fame and virtues of the great prior. The Medici, restored fourteen years after Savonarola's death, erected on the scene of his execution a magnificent fountain, in the vain hope that his name might be forgotten. Four hundred years have gone by, and, despite misunderstanding and calumny, the lustre of his fame shines more glorious than in the passing hour of his triumph. The storm of fierce passions which raged around him in life has forever subsided; pope and prince and politician who shared in his career have passed before the bar of eternal justice, where an everlasting seal has been set on the judgement divinely rendered. And though the judgement of history has not been finally pronounced, the mists of prejudice have been dissipated by the sun of truth, in whose clear light Savonarola, with all his faults, stands forth, assuredly a grand figure in the galaxy of the world's great men.

---

4   "O Rome, ungrateful country, thou shalt not even possess my bones!" Scipio Africanus's sad and indignant words we may apply for Savonarola to ungrateful Florence.

PART II

I

ESTIMATES OF CATHOLIC AND
NON-CATHOLIC WRITERS

✚

T O ESTIMATE THE character, the career, and the lasting work of Savonarola, is our purpose in this second part of our sketch. The Catholic histories of the Church in general use are by no means satisfactory guides when they discuss this important matter. Some are misleading; others are so inaccurate regarding the facts of Savonarola's life that their judgement of the man has little if any value.

Rohrbacher, in his *Universal History of the Church*, gives a very meagre account of the grave matters involved in the history of Florence during the last decade of the fifteenth century; but he does not hesitate, curtly and absolutely, to condemn Savonarola, alleging that the friar excused his disobedience to the Papal commands by adducing reasons he knew to be false. This verdict, it may justly be said, lacks the safeguards of sufficient testimony; it does not convey the whole truth; it is misleading. Deciding too much, it may be set aside as unjust. In comparing Savonarola to Ham, and then lashing him for exposing his father's ignominy (by his criticisms of Pope Alexander), Rohrbacher presents a forced illustration, a distorted figure, a mere trick of rhetoric. History's interests, as well as those of truth, are not conserved by such writing.

Darras is a popular author. Though neither thoroughness, nor wide learning, marks his four large volumes, yet he is much read by those who cannot go more deeply into church history. Dealing with Savonarola, Darras is not only misleading, but he is positively wrong as to the occasion of the prior's downfall. He pretends that Savonarola opposed the appeal of the conspirators who were executed, and that in consequence of the tumult that ensued in Florence, he was summoned to Rome. A reference to the facts and dates, as we have given them, will show how absurd this statement is, and how little "history" it contains.

Alzog's reputation for learning far exceeds that of Darras. But concerning Savonarola the German professor is not more satisfactory than the French abbé. Representing the prior as introducing the question of Florentine liberty at the bedside of Lorenzo, omitting all mention of the religious aspects of the supposed interview, and reducing the episode to a political encounter between the friar and the prince, Alzog is either woefully ignorant, or he wilfully distorts. His further statements that Charles VIII expelled Piero de' Medici that the Republic was "found impracticable;" that six conspirators were executed; the Dominicans caused the failure of the ordeal and that "it would seem that he [Savonarola] is not unfairly charged with being a forerunner of Luther," enable us to judge the value of Alzog on this subject. His closing remark that Savonarola's teaching was Catholic, and that it was a blunder to represent him as one of a group of "reformers" of the sixteenth century, contains not only a contradiction of the previous censure qualified censure— or—of the friar as a "forerunner" of Luther, but it is so inexact in expression, so unmindful of the accuracies which time and fact demand, that we dismiss it with a word of warning against such "history."

The distinguished Italian historian, Cesare Cantu, has sketched the life of the Ferrarese friar in the *Storia Universale*, and in the *Storia d' Italia*, as well as in *Gli Eretici d' Italia*. More studious, intelligent, and temperate than the writers we have just quoted, the judgement he passes is, nevertheless, defective, and one with which we are not in entire agreement. Savonarola, writes Cantu, was

> a man of faith, of superstition, of genius, abounding in charity. Contrary to Luther, who confided entirely in reason, he believed in personal inspiration. Arguments in his favour, as well as against him, may be drawn from his works, which, as a whole, evidence his attempt to harmonise reason with faith, Catholicity with political freedom. ... In no wise did he impugn the authority of the Roman See, although he resisted one whom he believed to be an illegitimate occupant of that See, and against whom he tried to invoke a Council which would reform the Church legitimately. Pride resulted from popularity, opposition induced excess; but he worked with a pure conscience, and without personal ambition. His opinions he endeavoured to propagate by example, and not by force; he believed in the efficacy of truth. ... Thinking to guide a mob by means of passion and of the hurly-burly of street crowds, he fell victim to one and the other, as commonly happens. ... The fame of Savonarola remains suspended between heaven and hell, but all deplored his death, and especially, perhaps, those who had caused it. ... Not one of the followers of the great friar figures among the disciples of Luther or among the betrayers of his country's liberty. Michelangelo, who raised bastions for his native city, and also the grandest church in Christendom, always venerated Savonarola.[1]

In the *History of the Papacy in the Fifteenth Century* Christophe appreciates the famous friar in the following words:

> Savonarola's eloquence is not that which comes from the use of the orator's arts, or from a depth of rea-

---

1 *Gli Eretici d' Italia*, Torino, 1865, vol. I., 234–235.

soning, or from an emotion agitating the orator's
self. It was an eloquence which seemed to despise all
human aids, and which, like the mystical figures of
Fra Angelico, aspires to heaven, and does not touch
the earth. . . . Savonarola is like no other orator. True
or pretended, he is a prophet; he has the visions, the
incoherence, the figurative language, the rashness
of one. For this reason, rather than by means of his
talent, great as it was, he captivated the multitude.
"Some make a fanatic, a sectarian, an impostor, of
Savonarola; others an apostle, a saint. The fact is,
there is something of all these in the Dominican. If
we open the door of his cell at St. Marco, and there
contemplate him at the foot of the crucifix, attenuat-
ed by fasting and wrapt in an ecstasy of prayer; if we
follow him to Santa Maria del Fiore, and hear him
reproaching voluptuous Florence with her vices, Savonarola is a saint, an apostle. But if we turn to the
other side, and behold the tribune who mixes politics
with religion, the declaimer who inveighs against the
existing powers, the seer who opposes a divine mission to the authority of the head of the Church, Savonarola is very like a fanatic, a sectarian, an impostor. Unfortunately he finished his life with the latter
character; such was the impression he made upon the
spectators when he left the scene; and we may well ask
ourselves whether, if he had preserved the popular favour, he would have anticipated the role of the monk
of Wittenberg. Protestants appear not to doubt it, for
they claim Savonarola as one of their forerunners.
But they forget that this monk broke the link which
might have connected him with their rebellion, on
the day, when, at the foot of the stake, he accepted
the absolution of the Pope, and handed down to posterity that tardy but solemn proof of his repentance.
. . . Savonarola knew not how to be either apostle or
saint. We would hesitate to call him a sectarian, and
we would dislike still more to style him an impostor.
We regard him as a sincere but prodigiously imag-
inative preacher. If we have studied him rightly, he
appears to have been carried away in the current of
an unregulated imagination from the day when he
began his prophetic exposition of the Apocalypse, to
that when he openly substituted for the authority of

the Church that of his own pretended celestial mission. Undoubtedly his eloquence is wonderful, but it is that of a vehement declaimer rather than that of a solid and enlightened teacher. We see in it the violent and convulsive agitation of a fever, rather than an effort of powerful and healthy thought. His energy does not warm, it burns, it boils over like the lava from a volcano. It does not illuminate, it dazzles; it does not guide, it impels. . . . His spirit cannot understand the positive side of things. Savonarola is seldom true; exaggeration seems to be his domain; his figures are colossal, his situations forced, his end greater than his means. We need not be surprised if a man so organised, with such a power of imagination and such weakness of sense, influenced by the enthusiasm which his words aroused, and by an idolatrous worship accorded him . . . —if such a man becomes intoxicated with himself and if he believes himself to be an envoy of the Lord. Savonarola succumbed to the hatred of factions which he had himself excited. In our days he would have succumbed to ridicule.[2]

Doctor Parsons, in his *Studies in Church History*, a work which is still in course of publication,[3] devotes a special chapter to Savonarola. In general the spirit displayed is one of fairness, though we deprecate the use of the word "agitator" as applied to the preacher. It is an undeserved reproach. This author treats the story of the trial of Savonarola with a scantiness that is very unsatisfactory. His statement that Savonarola demanded to be tried in Florence is not supported by the prior's letters. We find no evidence that he ever demanded a trial either at Rome, or Florence, or elsewhere. Nor can we agree with this author that much of the sympathetic interest which Savonarola's memory has evoked is attributable to the fact that the friar is a poetical figure, appealing to the imagination. And finally we take positive issue with the doctor when he declares that Catholics who have

2   With slight changes we adopt the translation printed by Doctor Parsons in his *Studies in Church History*.

3   [Editor's note: This work by Dr. Reuben Parsons was completed in 1906 three years after the death of Fr. O'Neil.]

praised Savonarola have been influenced by "the unhistorical and un-theological theory of a distinction between the Church and the Papacy."[4] We believe that a careful consideration of facts, as we have recorded them, will be a sufficient refutation of this rather sweeping charge.

The distinguished German historian of the Popes, Dr. Ludwig Pastor,[5] affords considerable space to Savonarola in the third volume of his learned work, in which he examines Pontiffs of the Renaissance period. With his estimate of the great prior many will probably agree, though we believe that occasionally his judgement is over severe, and we are certain that for some statements he fails to offer either good reasons or satisfactory authorities. He regards Savonarola as an extremist and a visionary, an opinion that ignores certain extraordinary facts not otherwise readily explained, if one wholly rejects the apposite theory of the preacher's genuine prophetic power. We agree with Doctor Pastor that Savonarola's fiery appeal for summary vengeance on all who would attempt the overthrow of the Republic was scarcely in keeping with the spirit which should ever actuate the priest; but should not his defect be condoned in view of the conditions and circumstances of the extraordinary affair? The charges that Savonarola admitted married women to the cloister without the consent of their husbands, that he encouraged espionage among children on their parents, among servants on their employers, that his rigorous methods occasioned family quarrels and divisions, are not sustained. We find nothing to justify these serious accusations.

Rather is the whole tenor of Savonarola's life their contradiction. Touching his relations with the Pope, Savonarola is judged in a Catholic spirit by Doctor Pastor, who says, however, that the friar failed to give the proof of a divine commission because, at

---

4   We have a warm feeling for Savonarola, but the distinction named we as warmly condemn, and so did Savonarola.

5   *Geschichte der Päpste in der Zeitalter der Renaissance*, Freiburg, 1895, Vol. III., 377–412.

a certain period, he refused to yield obedience. On this point we suggest that the historian's statement is not conclusive. As to events following Savonarola's failure in complete obedience to the Pope, we admit that the divine commission is not in evidence; as to Savonarola's previous labours, we do not see how a subsequent error could have vitiated their character, waiving all question of merit retained or lost. Moses assuredly had a divine commission, though at the close his slight fault was severely punished by God, Who withheld the temporal glory and crown. Admitting that worldliness in the Papacy culminated in Alexander, Doctor Pastor rightly contends, with St. Catherine of Siena, whom he quotes happily, that even if an incarnate devil sat in Peter's Chair, he must be obeyed—within his jurisdiction. We believe, however, with the German historian, that had Savonarola adopted more temperate measures towards the people of Florence, his success would have been more lasting. An excitable race, lacking depth of purpose, they were easily impressed. When the preacher's prophetic declarations were fulfilled, they hailed him as one sent of God; when his forebodings failed, they were only too ready to denounce him as a false guide.

Here it may be not amiss to quote the opinions of some of the friar's contemporaries. Of Machiavelli, Cesare Cantu says that, being a man who never risked the expression of an opinion contrary to that in fashion, he praised Savonarola in the beginning of his career.

> He began to ridicule the friar only when he himself had developed a polity that was directly opposed to the friar's—a polity, namely, without God, without Providence, without morality, an innate depravity, without original sin or redemption, by means of which he expected to restore Italy, not only without the Church, but in spite of her.

Machiavelli's history of Florence, ending with the death of Lorenzo, contains nothing about Savonarola. In an appendix, however, is published a letter from the author to a friend, in which he displays his feelings against the friar, whose sermons he had listened to. He accuses the preacher of fraud and cunning. In one of his "Discourses," however, he writes:

> The people of Florence are far from considering themselves ignorant and benighted, and yet Brother Girolamo Savonarola succeeded in persuading them that he held converse with God. I will not pretend to judge whether it was true or not, for we must speak with all respect of so great a man. But I may well say that an immense number believed it, without having seen any extraordinary manifestations that should make them believe it; but it was the purity of his life, the doctrines he preached, and the subjects he selected for his discourses, that sufficed to make the people have faith in him.

Elsewhere he says: "In the year 1491 Florence had reformed its government with the aid of Brother Girolamo Savonarola, whose writings exhibited much learning, intelligence, and courage."[6]

The celebrated Philip de Commines, who knew the friar well, speaks of him in the *Memoirs* as:

> A man famous for his holy life, and whom I myself saw and communed with in the year of our Lord 1495.... He led the holiest life that any man could lead, as appeared both by his conversation and also by his sermons, wherein he preached against all kinds of vice, so that he reformed the lives of many in the same city.... He told many things which proved true which he could not receive from the Council of Florence. And as touching the king, and the evils he said should happen to him, they came to pass as he prophesied; for first he told him of the dauphin, his son's death, and after of his own as myself can witness, for I have seen the letters he writ thereof to the king.

---

6   In his treatise *The Prince*, Machiavelli also refers to Savonarola, declaring that he failed simply because he tried to be a reformer without the use of material force. This Machiavellian principle finds its illustration in Mahomet and Luther; but the labours of those who, like Savonarola, "fought within the lines," have always been in ways of peace.

In the *History of Italy*, Guicciardini, who was only sixteen years old when Savonarola mounted the scaffold, presents the views of a supporter of the Medici.

The Pope, despised him [Savonarola], and exercised his spiritual arms more at the solicitations of some friars who hated Savonarola than from his own inclination. But Savonarola, finding that by his silence his interests declined and that the ends for which lie had preached could not be answered, began to despise the Pontifical Orders, and returned publicly again to his former office, asserting that the censures pronounced against him were null, as contrary to the Divine Will and public welfare, and at the same time inveighed bitterly against the Pope and the court of Rome. This occasioned frequent tumults; for his enemies, who gained ground every day, stirred up the populace, who above all things abhorred disobedience to the Pope, and had him reprimanded by some in the government for his audaciousness, which tended to alienate the Pope's affections from the Florentines at a juncture when he was treating with the allies for the restitution of Pisa. On the other hand, his followers alleged in his defence that it was dangerous to admit of an example which would be a precedent for Popes to intrude in the affairs of their government. These contentions lasted several days, till Alexander, in great wrath, issuing new Briefs, and threatening to interdict the city, the magistrates ordered him to desist from preaching. Savonarola obeyed, but the Dominican friars of his convent went from church to church, preaching the same doctrines, which were refuted by the religious of other Orders. These disputes were carried on with great heat, and excited animosities both in Church and state.

Savonarola was afterwards put to the Question,[7] but in a gentle manner, and his examination and confession were by the Magistracy formed into a process, and ordered to be published. In this paper, he cleared himself of several calumnies that had been laid to his charge, such as leading a dissolute life, being avaricious, and having kept secret correspondence with

7   That is, the torture

foreign princes. He confessed that those events he had foretold were not by Divine Revelation, but by his own proper opinion grounded on the doctrine of the Holy Scripture which he had profoundly studied; that what he had preached had not proceeded from any malignity, nor from any ambitious views of ecclesiastical preferments, but from zeal, and in hopes that through his means a general council might be assembled in which the corrupt manners of the clergy might be reformed, and the condition of the Church restored, so as to resemble as near as possible the apostolic times, in which laudable attempt if it had pleased God to help his labours, he should have thought himself more happy and glorious than if he had acquired the Popedom. For the first could not have been procured but by good sound doctrine and virtue, and a singular reverence gained from all men, whereas the other might be obtained, as it often was, by sinister means or good fortune.

Savonarola died with great intrepidity, without uttering a word concerning his guilt or innocence, leaving the passions of men unquenched, and their judgement uncertain. Some called him an impostor, whilst others affirmed that the confession published in his name was either false, or that what he had said had been extorted by the Question, a frailty which they excused, because the Prince of the Apostles, who was neither imprisoned nor forced by torments, at the interrogation of handmaids and servants, had denied being a disciple of that Master whose holy doctrine he had imbibed, and of whose many holy miracles he had been an eye-witness.

Without criticism of Guicciardini, whose prejudice will be apparent to the reader, we shall give a notion of the opinions of other contemporaries of the Frate, as Mr. Napier reports them:

Nardi, who although an impartial writer was no adherent of Savonarola, tells us at the end of his second book, how he is compelled from truth and conscience's sake to acknowledge that a great and noble citizen who had been one of the Frate's examiners and was appointed on account of his intense hatred, having been subsequently banished to his villa, was there questioned by the historian himself about Savonarola's confession and process, to which he answered in his wife's presence, "It is true that from the Fra Girolamo's confession certain things were omitted, with the best intention, and others added."

Giovanni Berlingheri also, who was one of the priors for March and April 1498, is said by Lorenzo Viole, a contemporary writer, to have preserved the original autograph confession of Savonarola, which Viole saw in part, compared it with the printed copies then in everybody's hands, and finally declared that "they differed as much as day and The truth was not written," he adds, "in these printed documents; but that only was inserted which they required to prove the Frate a wicked man, for the purpose of concealing their own injustice who had condemned an innocent one."

There were not wanting some worthy people, both before and after Savonarola's death, who endeavoured to persuade Berlingheri to publish this document, but in vain; and even on his death-bed, when his near relative Alessandro Pucci and his wife Donna Maria Sibilla implored him to give them the manuscript, he answered, "Neither to you nor to any person in the world will I show it, for my so doing might occasion the death of more than forty Florentine citizens, and God forbid that I should cause so much evil; have patience, for it would not be well that I should do this; nay, before I die I wish to cast it into the flames and see it burn."

Another actor in this tragedy, and a most important personage, Ser Francesco di Barone, a public notary, commonly called at that time "Ser Ceccone," who was believed to be the suggester and fabricator of the false process, is said to have confessed to Lucrezia de' Medici (Salviati), Leo the Tenth's sister, "that Savonarola was a saint of Heaven, but that it became necessary to impute crimes to him and feign many things in order to secure his condemnation..."[8]

8   *Florentine History from the Earliest Authentic Records to the Accession of Ferdinand III., Grand Duke of Tuscany*, by Henry Edward Napier, London, 1846-47, vol.

Finally, Magliabechi, a great authority and nearer our own times, exhibited proofs to his friends of the spurious process, which, according to Varchi, was subsequently expunged from the public records by the Proposto, Lorenzo Ridolfi, as disgraceful, unjust, and contrary to every rule of equity.

Among English writers of recent date, Madden deserves notice. In an exhaustive history of Savonarola, whom he calls "the intrepid Dominican," and "a great Christian hero," Madden holds that the friar

> appears to have been raised up by Providence at a crisis more terrible and perilous perhaps than any that preceded or followed it, to cry out against the iniquities that damaged the Church, and to combat the enemies within her gates, and those that beset her altars and her throne. He had to war with all kinds of treason against God, —covert heathenism in the name of Platonic philosophy simulating Christian principles; open disbelief in the government of a supreme power; speculative infidelity of schoolmen, secular and clerical, of rhetoricians and wrangling theologians; practical infidelity of churchmen who had become simonists and sensualists, enemies to truth and purity, and persecutors of just men believing in God and fearing His judgments. He died in the struggle, and the enemies of truth and justice thought they had a signal triumph. But his death only served to send his opinions, apostle-like, throughout the civilised world.

Briefly, in *Geschichten der Romanischen und Germanischen Völker von 1494 bis 1514*,[9] and most elaborately in the *Historisch-biographischen Studien*,[10] Leopold von Ranke has narrated the story of Savonarola's life. In the later volume he describes the rise of the Medici and the political variations in Florence, giving many details of the political revolution of 1494, and of Savonarola's

III., 617–620

9   Leipzig, 1574; Sämentliche Werke, vols, xxxiii., xxxiv.

10 Leipzig, 1887; see pp. 183–332.

leadership. The character of the new constitution introduced by the friar, the subsequent disturbances in Florence, the workings of European politics, Savonarola's complications, trial, and death, are all studiously set forth. To the political aims of the Frate he attributes an unusual importance, representing him as a partisan before his coming to Florence, and as working while there with an international party, to effect, through the aid of the French king, the forcible overthrow of Alexander VI. However, von Ranke is not unsympathetic. From the shorter sketch in the *Geschichten*, we extract some passages, fairly presenting the learned author's opinions:

> Among these rich, influential, educated, and solemn people [he had described the people of Florence], a Dominican, Hieronymus Savonarola of Ferrara, had succeeded in making himself universally esteemed. He was, it is true, strict with himself and others, a solitary walker, a monk by inclination, and a man who also knew how to control his harsh voice. He admonished his monasterial brethren to give up all their property. He spared no one, not one of his fellow-citizens, the Brescians, the Florentines, nor his liege lords, the Pope and Lorenzo de' Medici, and all this could not help securing him a certain influence. But what made him really powerful were, before all else, his doctrines and his prophetic gifts.

> He preached his theory that all true citizens ought to participate in the offices of public authority ... to many his scheme will appear nothing more nor less than an enlarged aristocracy. Savonarola was the head of all the enemies of the Italian League and the Pope. He condemned the wealth and the pomp of the clergy, for thereby the barrier was broken down which should separate the church and the world. . . . God's Word still endured, and by no means was one bound to trust in a prelate as much as in it. Nay, no one should sit in the seat of Doctrine except so long as his works were not prejudicial to the operation of the doctrine. Acting in accordance with these principles, he invited Charles orally, and the German and the Spanish kings in writing, to undertake the refor-

mation of the Church.[11]

Alongside von Ranke we place a Frenchman, M. Perrens, who, having studiously reviewed the friar's career, in *Jerome Savonarola, his Life, his Preaching, and his Times*, ventures to express a judgement on the man. Appreciating, as he says, successively, the statesman, the reformer, the theologian, the philosopher, the orator, the writer, in Savonarola, the puzzled reader asks was he a prophet or an impostor? The problem has been solved by historians in two extreme ways. On one side are those who condemn the Church in order to proclaim Savonarola a saint; on the other, those who rob Savonarola of his good name in order to protect the men whom he condemned for their shortcomings. "We must take," says Perrens, "a middle course. Savonarola was neither an angel nor a devil, neither a saint nor a reprobate, neither a prophet nor an impostor—*he was a man*." Perrens then proceeds, at considerable length, to illustrate his conclusion by citing the weaknesses, the contradictions, the faults, of Savonarola. He also enters into a long discussion to disprove Savonarola's prophetic character. He considers it to have been unfortunate for Savonarola that his appearance on the public stage began at a time when the work of political reform became confounded with the question of political reform in Florence, the latter impeding- the success of the former. Had Savonarola, M. Perrens opines, been a German, had he laboured in the field occupied later by Luther, the unhappy schism and heresy precipitated by the Wittenberg friar would have long been deferred.

The views of clerical Protestant church historians may not be unprofitable, so we turn to the well-known Dean Milman,[12] and quote from him at some length.

> Savonarola died, [so wrote his admiring biographer,] from this cause only, —because he was hated by the

11   Pages 85–92 of *Geschichten der Romanischen und Germanischen Völker*, etc.

12   *Savonarola, Erasmus and other essays*, Henry H. Millman, 1870, John Murray, London.

wicked, beloved by the holy.[13]

That he died because he was a preacher of righteousness, in an age and in a Church at the very depths
of unrighteousness, who will deny? His absolutely
blameless moral character, his wonderful abilities,
his command of all the knowledge of his time, his
power of communicating his own holiness to others,
even his rigid authority as regards the great doctrines
of his Church, who will impeach them? Let anyone
read in Italian, and he will not be unrewarded, the
Trionfo della Croce, and determine this point for himself. His other practical works, as on the simpleness
of the Christian life, if not of equal excellence, are as
faultless and devout.

We have not disguised what, from our point of view,
seems to detract from the grandeur, the heroic, the
saintly, the true Christian grandeur of Fra Girolamo.
It was a monkish reformation which he endeavoured
to work, and therefore a reformation which could
not have satisfied the expanding mind of man. But it
was the monkish reformation of a Church which still
professed to believe monasticism to be the perfection
of Christianity, a higher gospel than that of Christ.
We have touched on his extravagances of religious
passion, the rigour of his puritan asceticism. But not
only was he an Italian, he was of a church in which,
as witness the lives of half the saints (look especially to St. Francis), those extravagances had been held
up as the very consummation of holiness. If he was a
religious demagogue, and mingled too much in secular affairs, how many, not of the worst only, but of
the best, in the history of his Church would disdain
to elude the imputation! Above all he did not discern
the dim line which distinguishes the mission of a
preacher of righteousness from that of a prophet of
the future; he did not, in his ecstatic fervour of zeal,
discriminate between the ordinary and the extraordinary gifts of divine grace; yet his Church believed
herself to be endowed with a perpetual gift of mir-
acle, with a perpetual, if more rarely exercised, gift

---

13 "Una haec perditionis caussa Hieronymo, displicuisse nequissimis, placuisse
sanctissimis."—Pico Mirondola in Praefat.

of prophecy. How many who had prophesied smooth things of her, or even harsh things, had been canonised! It was not because they were untrue that Savonarola's predictions were presumptuous and impious, but because they were unwelcome. Had Charles the Eighth descended the Alps on the Pope's side, Girolamo's prediction had been a revelation from Heaven. We may believe the whole to have been hallucination, part of a fond perversion of unmeaning words by his partisans, part merely human sagacity, —some fortunate guesses or prophecies which wrought their own accomplishment, —but all their real criminality to Rome was their hostility to Rome. This was felt in his own day (the reaction was almost immediate); and it has been felt by the better part of the Roman Catholic Church at all times. There has been a strong demand for that highest homage to man, his canonisation, it was said to have been contemplated even by Julius II.; if we are to trust Dr. Madden, it has been thought of in our own time. How far it would tax theological subtlety to reconcile the excommunication and the murder of Savonarola (we can use no milder term) by one infallible Pope, with his sanctification by another, is no concern of ours.

"But Italy, Rome, the Church, repudiated the reformation, the more congenial and less violent reformation of Savonarola. A wider, more complete reformation—a reformation on different principles—became more and more necessary and inevitable. It was only by the reaction of the more formidable revolution of the North, that the South at length conformed to some of the views of the reformer of Ferrara."

[Here follows a little eulogy of Luther.]

Milman notes afterward that Savonarola's promise regarding the conversion of the Turks was not realised, and adds: "His political vaticinations were at least as sadly untrue, such as the promise to Florence of an age of unexampled prosperity after her tribulations." As to Savonarola's death he says: —"He died full of confidence in his own innocence, firm, calm, without the least acknowledgement of guilt, with no word of remonstrance against the cruelty of his enemies, at peace with himself, in perfect charity with all."

Dean Milman's views a reader may desire to compare with the Rev. Mr. Creighton's. While vicar of Embleton, this clever writer began a *History of the Papacy during the Reformation*. As each new volume appeared, of the six he has published, the author rose at least one step higher in the ministry, or the hierarchy, of the Established Church of England

> Savonarola's fate [says Mr. Creighton elegantly] is a type of the dangers which beset a noble soul drawn by its Christian zeal into conflict with the world. More and more he was driven to fight the Lord's battle with carnal weapons, till the prophet and statesman became inextricably entangled, and the message of the new life was interwoven with the political attitude of the Florentine Republic. Little by little, he was driven into the open sea, till his frail bark was swallowed by the tempest. He encouraged Florence to adhere to an untenable position till all who wished to bring Florence into union with Italian aspirations were driven to conspire for his downfall.

> This great tragic interest of the lofty soul, overborne in its struggle against the world, has made Savonarola a favourite character for biography, romance, and devotional literature. But the historical importance of Savonarola goes deeper than the greatness of his political importance. Savonarola made a last attempt to bring the new learning into harmony with the Christian life. He strove to inspire the Florence of Lorenzo, Ficino, and Pico with the consciousness of a great spiritual mission to the world. He aimed at setting up a commonwealth of which Christ was the only king: animated by the zeal of a reformed church, the state was to guide men's aspirations towards a regenerate life. The individual force and passion of Savonarola was the offspring of the Renaissance, but it had to force its way to expression through the fetters of scholasticism. Savonarola's sermons present a strong contrast of the forcible utterance of personal opinion with the trivialities of an artificial method of exposition. He palpitates with the desire to reconcile con-

flicting tendencies and enter into a larger world. He falls back upon the mysterious utterances of prophecy to point men's eyes to a larger future than he was able to define. His words are now vague to our ears, his political plans are seen to be dreams, his prophetic claims a delusion. But his character lives and is powerful as of one who strove to restore the harmony of man's distracted life.

It is unjust to Alexander VI to represent him as the chief author of Savonarola's ruin; but he gave his sanction at the last to the schemes of Savonarola's foes. It is needless to discuss the technical points at issue between Savonarola and the Pope; it is enough that the papal policy in Italy demanded the destruction of a noble effort to make Christianity the animating principle of life. Even a Pope so purely secular as Alexander VI is said in later years to have regretted Savonarola's death. Julius II ordered Raphael to place him among the doctors of the Church in the great fresco of the "Disputa," and his claims to canonisation were more than once discussed. The Church evidently grieved over his loss when he was gone, when political difficulties had passed away, and the memory of the fervent preacher of righteousness alone remained.[14]

As an illustration of the spirit animating Dominican historians, we present to our readers a few extracts embodying the judgement of several of the most distinguished members of the Order. Natalis Alexander, the celebrated Church historian, describes Savonarola as "a most fervent preacher, famous by the sanctity of his life, his doctrine, the gift of prophecies and miracles, who was hurried to his death by judges resolved on his destruction before they sat for his trial." The writer denounces the execution of Savonarola as most iniquitous.

Touron writes that "amongst the apostolic men in whose lives we have seen realised, all that our Lord foretold to his first disciples, the famous Jerome Savonarola holds high rank." After enumerating his great virtues and extraordinary labours, Touron

14   Creighton, M., *History of the Papacy*, vol. III., 247, 248.

continues, "The death of this truly great man was another proof
that he had spoken by the Spirit of God."

From Marchese, who was a patient student of every phase of
the Frate's life, we quote freely:

> The name of Savonarola arises from the infamy of
> the scaffold without injury; it will ever shine; it will
> be remembered with affection and reverence by Ital
> ians while religion and liberty remain dear to them.
> He was always true to himself in the innocence of
> his life, in the love of truth, in his charity towards
> mankind. It must be conceded that if he erred in the
> choice of means to attain his end, he had not, as some
> claim, an ambition for worldly power, or for any less
> noble purpose; his object was the elevation of a de-
> graded generation to the perfection of Christianity.

> No one, however, though among his most furious
> enemies, has ever dared to deny to him innocence
> and austerity of life, together with much and varied
> learning. Certainly, a most remarkable man he was,
> and deserving of honour, not only by his native Fer-
> rara but by Italy and the world. The pagans would
> have ranked him with Cato, and we may rank him
> with Athanasius the Great and Gregory VII. For, as
> Athanasius, though alone and unarmed, faced and
> conquered in his day Arius and his unusually pow-
> erful sect, and as Gregory scourged simony and the
> concubinage of the clergy, so Friar Girolamo, as long
> as he lived, fought reviving paganism.

> Among those of our times (the moderns), I find no
> one who resembles him so much as Daniel O'Con-
> nell, in common with whom he deserves praise for
> having tied in a sisterly knot true religion and true
> liberty. To some his social reform appears to be Uto-
> pian; but we should certainly bless a Utopia designed
> to make men virtuous and happy.

> During four centuries Europe has been engaged in a
> bloody battle to obtain a liberty which flies every hour
> before her; and when she believes she has reached it,
> she finds within her embrace only a painted strum-
> pet, —Licence. Savonarola loudly proclaimed that

there could be no real liberty without religion, and the guarantee of its rights consisted in the fulfilment of certain obligations. His warnings were derided; but we do not fear to affirm that Europe will never enjoy peace until these two truths are engrafted on modern civilization. To him who has not studied the interior history of those rugged and sensual times, Savonarola's impetuosity may seem supreme folly. But the holy Pontiff Adrian was not slow in amply justifying him, who in the Diet of Nuremberg desired the Nuntio Ceregato to confess freely before all the German princes that the Pope knew that the Lutheran heresy was an infliction from God especially for the faults of the priests and prelates, and therefore like unto that, as noted by Chrysostom, which Christ manifested in Jerusalem. The scourging began in the Temple, as He wished first to cure the head, rather than the members, of the infirm body. Such having been the gravity of the malady, the excessive zeal of Savonarola urged him beyond bounds of propriety in mode and speech, in which, nevertheless, he appears almost like the illustrious Bishop of Carthage, St. Cyprian, who with an equal impetus of inconsiderate zeal, and with a want of reason and an equal bitterness, publicly assailed the holy Pontiff St. Stephen; but who, as St. Augustine remarks, did not hesitate to cancel with his blood the fault that sprang rather from an error of the intellect than from a guilty desire. Thus, he did not lose the veneration of the faithful and of the Apostolic See, but he is deservedly held to be one of the most splendid lights of Christianity. Such a lot fell to Savonarola, who, placed amid the most difficult surroundings, gave heed to imprudent councils on the reformation of the Church; but his error was the result of sincere zeal, and was not due to ambition or to worldly cupidity.

Echard begins his comments on Savonarola by referring to the medals struck at Rome in 1510, in honour of the Prior of San Marco, and bearing the inscription, "Blessed Martyr and Doctor." The Holy See did not prohibit the sale or distribution of these medals.

"And deservedly," adds Echard, "does Savonarola receive these titles of honour; for his blameless life was spent in most fervent zeal and love of God, for the welfare of souls, and their advancement in virtue. Most wickedly rewarding this great man, ungrateful Florence brought him to the gibbet and the stake. By this they thought to attach infamy to his name; on the contrary, however, it has become more illustrious with advancing time. Not only have the books which he published during his active labours been preserved and further disseminated, but those works which he composed when in prison are also issued for the relish and advantage of all who read them."

Echard maintains that the trial of Savonarola was a mockery of justice, that the Florentines, finding no cause, either civil or ecclesiastical, for which they could condemn him, put him to death for political reasons only, covering these under false charges of heresy and of prophetical imposture. To these varying estimates of the illustrious Ferrarese, expressed at different periods, by men wide apart in their calling and in their creed, it pleases us to add the judgement of a mind so acute and so religious as that of Cardinal John Henry Newman [Now canonised]. In his sermon on the Mission of St. Philip, Cardinal Newman depicts Savonarola as

> a true son of St. Dominic in energy, in severity of life, in contempt of merely secular learning; a forerunner of St. Pius the Fifth in boldness, in resoluteness, in zeal for the honour of the house of God, and for the restoration of holy discipline. He felt his spirit stirred up within him, like another Paul, when he came to that beautiful home of genius and philosophy; for he found Florence like another Athens, wholly given to idolatry. He groaned within him, and was troubled, and refused consolation, when he beheld a Christian court and people priding itself on its material greatness, its intellectual gifts, and its social refinements, while it abandoned itself to luxury, to feast and song and revel, to fine shows and splendid apparel, to an impure poetry, to a depraved and sensual character of art, to heathen speculations, and to forbidden,

superstitious practices. His vehement spirit could not be restrained, and got the better of him. He burst into a whirlwind of indignation and invective, which for the moment certainly did a great deal more than St. Paul was able to do at the Areopagus. St. Paul only made one or two converts there, and departed; whereas Savonarola had great immediate success, frightened and abashed the offenders, rallied around him the better disposed, and elicited and developed whatever there was of class. piety, whether in the multitude or in the upper It was the truth of his cause, the earnestness of his convictions, the singleness of his aims, the impartiality of his censures, the intrepidity of his menaces, which constituted the secret of his success.[15]

---

15   The student may further consult Muratori's *Annals*, Sismondi's *Italian Republics*, the work of Dr. Clark, or Mr. J. S. Harford's *Life of Michelangelo Buonarroti*.

II

The True Character of the Friar

✠

HAVING PLACED BEFORE our readers the estimates of Savonarola formed by various writers, Catholic and non-Catholic, at different periods, we may briefly present the true character of the friar.[1] He was a man of "most rare

---

1 Savonarola's full baptismal name was Jerome Mary Francis Matthew. A description of his personal appearance will be of interest to our readers. From the metrical "Cedrus Libani" by F. Benedict, we render one stanza literally:

"He was small of body, but very healthy,
His limbs were rather delicate,
His holy hand seemed transparent.
Ever joyous, never disturbed, His glance was quick, penetrating.
His expression was pleasing,
His eye beautiful,
His hair was wavy and black.
His mouth was large, his nose arched;
When his soul lighted up his face
It shone with such beauty and grace.
That he seemed to have come from Heaven."

From this description, and from the accounts left by Burlamacchi and Pico della Mirandola, we may state that Savonarola was of middle height and slight figure, graceful in movements, refined in his manners, of a nervous temperament, a believer in the doctrine of "cleanliness next to godliness." He had an orator's mouth and a nose such as belongs to all great men. His general expression was one of gravity, meditation on serious things having left its indelible traces. His likeness proclaims a "homely" man; but nobility of character, gentleness united with

virtues. He was benignant and pleasant with all, humble and gentle with his novices, of great affability. His agreeable manners gave joy and gladness to others. Those who once came to know him felt the strongest desire and eagerness for his company; and when he discoursed on spiritual things, no one who heard him would withdraw from his presence."[2]

He was a man of frequent prayer, of deep meditation, of constant study of Holy Writ. Knowing the Bible thoroughly, he made it the well-spring of his spiritual instructions, and even applied it to political affairs by way of interpretation and adaptation of figures. Some of the copies of the inspired Book which he read and annotated are still preserved. They bear striking testimony to his great learning, wonderful spirituality, and intense Catholicism. Not a single text which Luther or his followers distorted from the hitherto accepted meaning received from Savonarola aught but the most faithfully Catholic comment. Savonarola professed and practised, as a true Dominican, a most tender devotion to our Lady. He was a disciple of the Cross, on whom the seal of suffering had been early set.[3] His love for our Lord in the Holy Eucharist was a marked characteristic of his spiritual life. In the chapel he was often known to spend hours in prayer, rapt at times as if in ecstasy; a radiant flood of light was often visible to those who witnessed his fervour. While celebrating Mass his face was illumined, as with the fire of his love, and in consequence of this prodigy he was accustomed to seek the privacy of such altars as hid him from all save his attendant.

firmness, a certain melancholy sweetness, are clearly outlined. Various portraits of Savonarola are in existence, among them one on canvas by Fra Bartolomeo in the Academy of Fine Arts, Florence; a fresco in Savonarola's cell, also by Fra Bartolomeo; a third, an intaglio, by the celebrated engraver on gems, Giovanni della Corniola, now in the Uffizi Gallery, Florence. Another cameo by the same artist was in the possession of the Jesuits at Rome when Marchese wrote.

2   Burlamacchi, *La vita del beato Ieronimo Savonarola*.

3   "We cannot state whether Savonarola knew of the prophecies alleged to have been made concerning him which we find recorded in Burlamacchi. We refer especially to one by a canon of the Duomo, Prospero Petti, who was explicit in his declaration as to a Dominican who was destined to suffer and die for ungrateful Florence. The report and presentation of such prophecies are at least an evidence of the exalted state of feeling prevailing among Savonarola's followers."

His religious life was one of loyal observance of vows and rules. Truly detached from the world, single in his aims, pure in his motives, a model of simplicity, which neither learning nor honours ever disturbed, an example of humility, fortified by true courage accompanied by an utter disregard of human respect, he wore his white habit in honour to the end. As a superior he lived among the members of his community, a model of every virtue, a tender father watching over his beloved children with unfailing care.[4] His priesthood was one sustained, brave, generous effort to bring souls to God. Enjoying an extraordinary insight into the human heart, his influence as a confessor, director, or spiritual guide, was remarkable. As a preacher, he ranks among the greatest of all time. Judged by his success he may be considered a prince among orators. Sustained by unimpeachable honesty, by a devotion that even his enemies could not deny, by a learning that the scholars of the day were compelled to admire, fired by the conviction of a divine mission, a conviction in which his hearers shared unquestioningly,[5] his eloquence had a matchless

4   Burlamacchi has left a picture of the family life of St. Mark's community under the direction of Savonarola that reveals the great man in the true light of religious simplicity:
"After the siesta, the brethren would gather around the Father, in cheerfulness and eagerness, to hear some passage of Holy Writ explained. While they walked in the garden he would comment on the sacred text, thus mingling innocent recreation with pious meditation. Sometimes he would take the life of a saint for the subject of his discourse; again they would sing joyous hymns. At other times he would bid them dance, accompanying them by the humming of an appropriate air. A practice often followed was that of robing a young novice to represent the Divine Child. Then they would sit around him, giving, as to the beloved Jesus, their hearts, and asking graces for themselves and others."
Another picture, beautiful and touching, is that of the Father surrounded by his "angels," the dear young boys whom he loved to train for the heavenly life, going abroad in the fields, and having indulged in that godly hilarity which has ever been a virtue with religious, resting briefly in the pleasant shade of the trees. On one of these occasions, he entertained the brethren by taking from the tender branches their pith, and deftly and artistically forming it into little doves which he distributed among his angels as symbols of their innocence and purity. On such features, the inner life of Savonarola, it would be delightful to dwell, for the world knows him chiefly as the preacher, the reformer, the man mighty in word, and strong in the battle for right.

5   The claim that an angel was at times seen near him when he preached, and again a dove, we mention as a proof of the enthusiastic reverence of his followers, without vouching; for its truth.

influence, day after day, during the years he preached, swaying intellect and heart alike, ruling as from a throne the young and old men even more notably than women, and exercising what has not inaptly been termed a "*heavenly despotism*" over a city in which vice and irreligion had formerly established a stronghold.[6] As a prophet Savonarola's place cannot be determined with accuracy. Many of his predictions were fulfilled. In what spirit he made all of these we cannot decide, whether as a keen reader of the times, a close student of events, or as a man directly under the divine influence; but we readily understand how so many who heard him, and so many who have only read his words, should believe that he enjoyed a special heavenly assistance. The natural enthusiasm of his disposition, the impetuosity of a zeal, that perhaps needed, at times, the reign of greater caution, the warmth of his splendid imagination fired to a hot glow by meditation, by contemplation of the Apocalyptic prophecies and the books of the Old Testament, may have led him to make applications,

---

6   "As a political orator he was scarcely inferior to Demosthenes and Cicero. These two appeared when Greece and Rome were corrupted and divided, their liberty menaced by insidious and powerful enemies. They defended and sustained their country by the power of their eloquence. The wealth, the arms, the subtlety of Philip of Macedon had no more stubborn opponent than the eloquence of Demosthenes inspired by patriotism. In the same way Piero de' Medici vainly attempted with gold, arms, and snares, to oppress his country, once the eloquence of Savonarola fired the hearts of the Florentines with love for religion and liberty. Regarding the conspiracy of Bernardo del Nero, Savonarola resembles Cicero, who discovered and punished the wicked plots of Catiline and of his abandoned satellites. Savonarola, if not with arms, certainly with the word, preserved Florence for a long time from the conspiracies of the Medici and the Compagnacci. There was no lack of such plotters against liberty. As Cicero chastised the rapine of Verres and the gilded vices of Vatinius and of Crassus, so Friar Girolamo scourged those of the Sforzas, the Medici, and of the degenerate clergy. Savonarola differed from Demosthenes in this: The Greek orator bound in a confederation all the cities of Greece, opposing them to the Macedonian armies; whereas Girolamo dissuaded the Florentines from the League, which alone could debar the entrance to the enemies of Italy, preferring rather the safety of Florence than the uncertain results of the League. Demosthenes, being condemned to banishment and death, voluntarily shortened his days with poison. Cicero, however, was a victim more like the friar. As Caesar Octavius, who was loved by Cicero, bought the friendship of Marc Antony, thus sacrificing his own benefactor, so the Florentine politicians, thinking to gratify Alexander the Sixth, sacrificed Savonarola. I shall not attempt a further comparison between the Greek and Ionian orators and Savonarola. I shall only say that nature probably endowed Savonarola with eloquence as great as that with which she enriched Demosthenes or Cicero." —Father Marchese, O.P.

especially to Florence, in a manner not altogether undeserving of adverse criticism. But allowing for all these probabilities, one may be tempted to hold that, occasionally, he was granted an extraordinary light.

As a politician Savonarola has been most severely censured, though not always with reason. He deserves no condemnation for loving true liberty, the liberty of Christianity; nor for desiring that this spirit of liberty should influence the domain of civil government; nor for attempting to reform the citizens of Florence morally, thus ensuring the political welfare of the state. His ideal, originally, was beautiful: to build up a kingdom of love, mercy, and peace ; and this ideal he presented to the people continually. Thanks to the friar, Jesus Christ was King of Florence for two years at least; King over all in name, and over many in truth. "Why," says Villari, "should Savonarola be robbed of his fame as a statesman, when we behold a people called back to life, as it were, by his breath, and see that the government he framed is the admiration of all writers, both in old times and new?"[7] Around this wonderful man there gathered three groups of supporters, —one filled with deep conviction and holiest purpose, and to the indiscretion of some of whom, no doubt, a portion of Savonarola's troubles may be imputed; another that felt, in a superficial way, the religious influence of the preacher; and a third whose only motive was political ambition, or sordid gain. However much we admire Savonarola, we cannot be blind to his mistakes and defects. The selfish and imprudent advice and encouragement that he too freely accepted from this third class of supporters, misled him. Unconsciously he became an active politician, thus assuming a role seldom, if ever, becoming of a cleric. As a preacher, occupying a lofty position, expounding principles of government, even though his plan was Utopian,

7   "Savonarola was no demagogue," writes Dinwiddie. "He was as much alive to the evils of an unguarded democracy as he was to those of an oligarchy or an absolute monarchy; and his great design was to secure the establishment of a just, well-ordered and stable government, which should promote both the earthly and the spiritual welfare of the community."

condemning vice among public men especially, and pleading for the reign of justice and of morality, his position was dignified, sound, and sure.[8]

8　　Some notion of his teachings may be gained from the following extracts: "If you have heard it said that states are not governed with Pater Nosters (a remark attributed to Cosimo de' Medici), remember that this is the theory of tyrants, of men who are the enemies of God, and of the common weal, —a theory devised to oppress, and not to elevate and free the state. On the contrary, if you would have a good government, you must return to God. If it were not so, I should certainly not trouble myself about the state." "O my people!" he exclaims, "you know that I have never wished to enter into the affairs of the state; think you that I should do so now if I did not see that it was necessary for the safety of men's souls? You would not believe, but now you see, that my words are all proved true; that they are not mine, but that they come from the Lord. Give ear, then, to one who seeks only your salvation. Purify your hearts, give heed to the common good, forget private interests; and if you thus reform your city in this disposition, it will be more glorious than it has ever before been."

"What have you given me for trying to govern you? Where are the presents you have sent me? O Friar, you say, you have thousands of ducats! If anyone says so, he does not speak the truth; I have nothing, and I want nothing. It is you who want to be first (referring to the aristocratic obstructors of the proposed constitution), and that is your reason for disliking the council. He who wants to be first seeks to overthrow the government of the whole people; he will have no magistrates nominated without his permission; he must be consulted about everything, even to the appointment of a priest to the Church of Santa Reparata [the patron saint of Florence]. For my part, I endeavour to maintain the council. Accuse me no more, then, of wanting to rule your city. Christ alone, I tell you, is your King!"

How admirable is the following: "Well, Florence, God is willing to satisfy thee, and to give thee a Head, a King, to govern thee. This King is Christ. The Lord will govern thee Himself if thou wilt consent, O Florence! Suffer thyself to be guided by Him. Do not act as did the Jews when they required a king of Samuel. God said to Samuel, 'Hearken unto the voice of the people in all that they say unto thee; for they have not rejected thee, but they have rejected Me, that I should not reign over them.' O Florence, do not imitate this people! Take Christ for thy Master, and remain subject to His law.

"Magistrates," he says, "it is to you that I address myself. Put down these vices, destroy these sins, punish this horrid passion which is against nature. And not merely by a private fine, but in public, that all Italy may know it. Expose all the courtesans in a public place, and send them off to the noise of trumpets. But you say, O Father! There are so many of them that this would be to upset the whole city. Well, then begin with one, then go on to the rest; and if you cannot give them chastity, you can at least teach them decency."

"Punish gamblers; for be well assured gambling still goes on. Give orders, Signors, that no one shall play in the streets at great games or small. Have the tongues of blasphemers pierced. St. Louis, King of France, had the lips of the blasphemer cauterised, and said, 'I should have been happy to have as much done to myself, if I could at such a price have my kingdom cleared of such offenders.' Put down dancing, too, for this is not a time to dance. Prohibit balls in town and country." He refers here to the penitential season. The playing he would interdict was not of pastime, but of gambling.

Once, however, that he sided with a political faction, he ran risks, —the risk of envies, jealousies, calumnies, and the common risk that all simple men run, the risk of base ingratitude, the risk of being sacrificed by greedy fellows who no longer accounted him useful. And indeed such was the Frate's painful experience. Seeing him in the pulpit, honoured, powerful, a master, who would have dreamed of seeing him on a scaffold, neglected, despised, helpless.[9]

9   The esteem in which the Prior of San Marco was held in his own convent, may be measured by the remarkable fact, noted by Bzovius, that, of the eighty novices there at the date of his execution, not one returned to the world, nor did one go over to the Roman, or to the Lombard, province. Among his most bitter opponents, more than one was touched by remorse after the Frate's death. Touron tells us that Fra Mariano, repenting his enmity, publicly acknowledged his error, stating that, of his own knowledge, Savanarola was a man of extraordinary virtue and the recipient of rare heavenly favours. Ludovico the Moor, according to Bzovius. acknowledged, during his imprisonment in France, that Savonarola had been grossly calumniated, in order that his ruin might be more surely effected.

III

HIS INFLUENCE ON CHRISTIAN
EDUCATION, LITERATURE, AND ART

✠

ON EDUCATION, LITERATURE, and art the influence of Savonarola was mighty, truly beneficial, and pre-eminently Catholic; yet in the "Introduction to the Literature of Europe in the Fifteenth, Sixteenth, and Seventeenth Centuries," Hallam does not even mention the name of this great man However, there is no lack of authorities. From the splendid work of M. Rio, *Du Vandalisme et du Catholicisme dans L'Art*, we shall make a few extracts. The name of this author, who was a staunch Catholic of La Vendee, and a professor of history in the Royal College of Louis the Great, is well known to scholars. This distinguished Frenchman, whom Montalembert congratulated for having "reconquered for the Church the glory and genius of Savonarola," devoted a considerable portion of his great book on Vandalism and Catholicism in Art to a vindication of the illustrious Prior of San Marco, M. Rio says: "Not to recognize in Savonarola the powerful dialectician, the accomplished orator, the profound theologian, the bold and far-reaching genius, the universal philosopher, or rather the competent judge of all the schools and systems of philosophy, would be giving the lie with too much effrontery to history and to his contemporaries." The man thus gloriously endowed, whose sentiments on the true, the good, the beautiful, are scattered as gems through his discourses, proclaiming him at once poet and artist, was also crowned with virtues that were the most precious fruits of a truly religious life. With this splendid equipment, Savonarola stood forth as the champion of the Christian school, Christian literature. Christian art.

"Nothing less," again we quote M. Rio, "than supernatural assistance was required to purify all that paganism had defiled; for there was not a single branch of the sciences or of the arts, not a single faculty of the human mind, that had escaped the contagion. By dint of prostrating themselves before this ancient idol, men had come, at last, to be ashamed of the ignominy of the Cross; and Burlamacchi tells us that Savonarola found Florence full of those who, while adorned by noble birth and genius, and rich in the treasures of human wisdom, had not only lost their faith, but even derided those who kept it, and still more, those who defended it. There were artists of the highest grade who declared boldly that they had never had the faith; and amongst those who kept more within bounds to avoid scandal, the profession of Christianity was confined most frequently to some external observances. The teachers who had the charge of public education fed the minds of the youth, for the most part, only with a poisoned diet, systematically turning their admiration towards the fables of the Greek mythologies, or the heroes of the ancient republics, and not permitting them even to suspect that Christianity had her heroes too who had surpassed them all."

This is a sad, a humiliating picture, but it is only a hint, a suggestion. In general terms, M. Rio describes the condition of affairs confronting the great preacher and teacher, but he does not go into details. Contemporary chronicles assure us that the craze of the revival of letters so possessed teachers and parents in the second half of the fifteenth century that paganism's worst "literature" was set before the little ones, — the licentious verses

of Tibullus, Catullus, and Ovid, besides certain eclectic compila-
tions that were the very refuse of heathen filth. These abominable
methods, followed in what we would call primary and grammar
schools, were developed in philosophy and even in theology, as
taught in the universities. The shadow of paganism rested on the
holiest treasures of Catholic intellectual life. As we have already
remarked, the Gospels were Platonised. The terminology of some
writers, even ecclesiastics, was so blasphemously degraded that
they spoke of nuns as Vestales, vestals of the Blessed Virgin as
Diva the goddess, of our Blessed Lord as Minerva springing from
the head of Jupiter, etc.

It was against this flood-tide of iniquity that Savonarola put
forth his splendid strength. With an utter disregard of human
respect, he fearlessly arraigned false teachers occupying places
high or low. He thought tenderly and anxiously for the children,
on whom he rested his hopes, and for whom he pleaded with the
parents. His sermons also abound in passages addressed directly
to the little ones, in which his marvellous power is won The
duties of father and mother in the education of their children he
discussed with great earnestness and clearness. A friend of true
classical scholarship, he deprecated only the vile, the degrading. He saw beyond mere form; and though he would not exalt
the less perfect Latin or Greek of the Fathers as contrasted with
the Pagan writers of the golden ages of antiquity, he eloquently
maintained that substance and truth must not be forgotten.[1]
Thus, while approving the polish which comes of classic finish,
he strenuously insisted on the solid culture which only truth can
generate; and so he demanded that with Homer and Virgil and
Cicero, the Christian fathers, a St. Jerome, a St. Ambrose, and a
St. Augustine, should be studied. He would balance the lessons

1 "It is well known," says Symonds, "that Savonarola's objection to classical
culture was based upon his perception of its worldliness." And in confirmation
of Savonarola's view as to the Pagan tendencies of his time, Symonds quotes a
passage from Erasmus, who expressed his fear that the culture of the Renaissance
period would be the occasion of a revival of paganism among those who held to
Christ only in name, their spirit being with the heathen. Melanchthon was of the
same opinion.

of Plutarch's great men by the inspiring story of Christian hero-
ism and sanctity in every walk of life. The evil which Savonarola
combated so energetically, and for a time so successfully, in the
lower schools, was of monstrous growth in the academies and
universities. Into the cloisters, too, that spirit had penetrated,
and even some members of his own community had not entirely
escaped the tendencies of the times. The power of the pulpit had
not been uniformly used for Christian education; rather many
of the clergy were indifferent to it because they aspired to be
classical according to the fashion.

Can we wonder that at such a time and under such conditions
literature was corrupt in its substance and influence and that
artists were wanting in faith? Must we not deplore the downward trend of morals, and even of faith, among the youth grad-
uated from such schools, and whose subsequent intellectual
life was determined and moulded, to a great extent, by the lectures, books, paintings, sculptures, that were the productions
of a neo-pagan culture? Assuredly Christian taste was vitiated;
Catholic instincts suffered grievously; the sanctuary of the home
was defiled, and the house of God profaned.

It needed a man of splendid courage, of heroic virtue, to
attack the monstrous evil. Savonarola did not hesitate. Poet,
scholar, and lover of the arts, the calumnious shafts of his enemies — enemies of virtue and faith — fall harmless, though
rained against him in a very shower by the Pagans of his own
day, and by the bigots of succeeding times.[2] True history absolves
from all taint of iconoclasm the noble friar who stood alone,
while Italy idly beheld his dauntless struggle against the multitude, "to re-establish the reign of Jesus Christ in the hearts
and souls of the people; to enlarge and extend the blessings of
redemption to all the human faculties and to all their operations.

---

2   The Rationalist historian, Villari, says pointedly: "While regarded by sceptics
and pedants as one bent on reviving the past, Savonarola was held by great souls
of Michelangelo's stamp to be, as he truly was, the precursor of a new era, in
which the power of Christianity would again he revived without prejudice to
nature or antiquity."

The enemy that he combated, with all the energy of his soul and all the power of his word, was paganism, of which, as we have said, he had everywhere found traces, —in arts and morals, in ideas as well as acts, in the cloisters as well as in the schools of his age."[3]

Savonarola may also be reckoned among the reformers of philosophy. Opposing the tendency which leaned excessively to the authority of Aristotle, and combating the abuses then prevalent in scholastic philosophy, he raised this study to a higher plane by adapting the methods and principles of St. Thomas, whom he called "the Giant," to the issues and needs of his day. In his *Apology for the Art of Poetry*, Savonarola made a conclusive answer to his critics. This treatise embodies the thoughts and sentiments which he frequently expressed in his sermons, and is a beautiful exposition of the true and the good. He denounces false poets, and defends himself cleverly against their charge that he is an enemy of poetry, because he has ridiculed rhymesters who called themselves poets, knowing only the turn of a dactyl or a spondee, and whose "babbling, lawless productions" forebode for genuine scholars the "coming of the age, not of iron, but of tinsel and gossamer." He had excited the anger of these scribblers when he revived among the people the old songs, and set them, with patriotic fervour, against the licentious ballads then prevailing.

While enemies attacked him, and left their diatribes as a basis of calumny to succeeding ages, the success of Savonarola's crusade was acknowledged by many of the literary celebrities who were his contemporaries. "I do not think," writes M. Rio, "that there has ever been a hero in history whose name has been transmitted to posterity with a more imposing escort of men illustrious in every department; and we can hardly persuade ourselves that we are dealing with nothing but a simple friar, when we read the enumeration of the philosophers, the poets, and the artists of every kind,—architects, sculptors, painters,

3   M. Rio., *Du vandalisme et du Catholicisme dans l'art*, 1839, Debécourt, Paris.

and even engravers,—who offered themselves to him, almost in a body, with enthusiasm, to serve, each in his own sphere, as a docile instrument of the great social reformation."

Thus, Ficino became his apologist and resolved to give the remainder of his life to religion. The famous Benevieni was a most energetic defender of his doctrines and prophecies. Pico della Mirandola sold his property, gave the proceeds to Savonarola for the poor, and sought the habit of St. Dominic, in which he was buried. Politian, the most learned man of letters in his day, also asked the favour of the Dominican habit as he lay on his death-bed. The famous Nicholas of Schomberg, professor in the University of Pisa, abandoned his chair, followed the great prior to San Marco, and subsequently rose to the episcopacy and the cardinalate. These are only a few of the more notable among the many that felt and acknowledged the powerful genius of the man who was the apostle of Christian education. Christian literature. Christian art, in the very citadel of neopaganism; who stemmed the tide of the Renaissance, diverting its flood into safe channels, and preventing, in a measure, the excesses which lie could not overcome, and which culminated in an age miscalled "golden," and under a Pontiff whose brother Savonarola had driven from the city but lately ruled by their father, Lorenzo the Magnificent.[4]

---

4   Referring to the "blasphemers," as she too vigorously designates the assailants of Savonarola as an enemy of the arts, Mrs. Oliphant speaks of the glory of San Marco, the Convent of the Blessed Angelico and Fra Bartolommeo: "No other monastic institution has had such a double crown, and it is curious to find the home and centre of the great mission of Savonarola— he who was the burner of vanities, and the enemy, as his enemies say, of the beautiful—thus nobly distinguished by art."
For an interesting account of the influence exerted by Savonarola on the artists of his time, see *Lives of the Most Eminent Painters, Sculptors, and Architects of the Order of St. Dominic,* by the Dominican, Father Marchese. This valuable work was translated into English by the Rev. C. P. Meehan, and published by James Duffy, Dublin, in 1852. The reader of these volumes will also find the names of the illustrious artists who, through Savonarola's influence, joined the Dominican Order during his lifetime and after his death.

IV

SAVONAROLA AND LUTHER

✠

W E NOW COME to the question of Savonarola's faith, and to the charge that he was a forerunner of Luther. The assumption that the Prior of San Marco anticipated the German friar, and sought to "reform" the Church after the manner of the northern heretic, rests on two counts: (1) He is accused of teaching the pet doctrine of Luther, justification by faith without good works;[1] and (2) he is ranked with those who have denied the supremacy of the Holy See. A brief examination of the first count will be sufficient, but we shall re-enforce the refutation by a few reflections. The second count we shall consider in the next division of this chapter.

A contrast of the two men in their personal life and in the results of their work cannot fail to be instructive. The character of Savonarola we have already seen, —beautiful in faith, in piety, in good works, in loyalty to his vows as a religious. He laboured for the elevation of his Order to a greater fidelity to rule and

---

1   When Villari, Sismondi, and others speak of "the new doctrine" of Savonarola, they mean the newness of life, the moral regeneration which he introduced in Florence, not a change in articles of faith. A misunderstanding or a perversion of this fact we have observed in many Protestant writers.

observance, and for the transformation of private and public
life in Florence. Hear the testimony of one of his opponents who
wrote: "To me indeed (and the same is admitted by everyone)
the city seems much changed from that which I formerly knew.
It is daily becoming more like a second Nineveh; for just as the
latter converted itself to God at the preaching of Jonas, so also
does the former at the exhortation of our preacher."

Verily this was a true reform of men and manners. Luther
inaugurated his "reform" by violating his solemn vows, and
by inducing a nun to commit the same sacrilege. His gluttony,
drunkenness, and grossness in various ways are a scandal to
humanity. As to his work, we let himself speak:

> Since we have begun to preach our new doctrine the
> devil triumphantly walks about, the world grows
> daily worse, more impious, more shameless. Men are
> more avaricious, more impure, than they were under
> the Pope. Everywhere we find abominable passions,
> —drunkenness, immodesty, disgraceful disorders,
> schisms, sects, complete ruin of order and moral-
> ity. Licence and vice are carried to such excess that
> people know no check ; they live without shame, as
> untamed beasts, a prey to every vilest pleasure." And
> again: "Now everybody, anybody, knows the Gospel
> better than Dr. Luther, or even St. Paul himself. No-
> bles, citizens, peasants, despise the pastors of God, or
> rather the God and Master of pastors."

How sad a picture! How accurately did Montaigne sketch it
when he wrote in the essay on "Physiognomy" his denunciation
of "reformation by the utmost of deformations." And of the
man who precipitated this ruin, let his friends speak. Zwinglius
declares that the devil had so far mastered Luther that it fore-
boded his entire possession. Melanchthon wrote that he trem-
bled when he thought of Luther's passions, which yielded not in
violence to those of Hercules. Oecolampadius said that he was
seduced by Satan, being full of pride and arrogance, and another
cried out against him as a madman ever combating truth. "How

disgusting are his morals," was the complaint of the new church established at Zurich; "his words seem to be those of the devils who carry him along."

In his history of Charles the Fifth, the Scotch Protestant, Robertson, says of Luther: "His doctrines encouraged, and his life set the example, of the utmost licentiousness of manners." This unfortunate man, an acknowledged drunkard, whose immoralities shocked even licentious followers, whose advice to Melanchthon, "sin boldly, but have more faith than sin," is an appalling blasphemy, stands before the world as the leader of "reform," and is acknowledged and even reverenced by many (despite the palpable contradiction involved in resting their faith on the authority of one whose fundamental teaching was the rejection of all authority save that of private, personal judgement) as the originator of a great and heavenly blessing to humanity. He feigned that Savonarola was his forerunner, and in proof of his absurd claim perverted the prior's truly Catholic teaching, when he published in German some of the latter's commentaries on the Psalms.[2]

The linking of the name of such a man to that of the pure and devout Savonarola assuredly can not be attempted on personal grounds. If any ties exist, they must be of theory, for the practical effects of their doctrine were wholly dissimilar. In his commentaries on the Thirtieth and Fiftieth Psalms, written in prison, Savonarola speaks of faith and good works. A passage was wrested from its just meaning, and a forced interpretation put upon it, not only by Luther when he published these treatises at Strasbourg in 1524, and hailed Savonarola as a forerunner who had placed all justification in faith, but also by many writers since Luther's time.[3]

"It is absolutely false," says the Protestant Professor Villari, "that he ever renounced or neglected to maintain the value of

2   Consult Appendix I.

3   Notably the German biographers of Savonarola, Rudelbach (1835), Meier (1836), Hale (1851), all of whom signally failed to sustain their plea.

good works and religious ceremonies." The tenor of his whole life proves this; his last writing in prison, the remembrance to his jailer, confirms his unwavering Catholic doctrine. "Therefore," he concludes, "perseverance in virtuous living, in good works, in Confession, in Communion, in all that draws us nearer to grace, is the true and certain way to procure its increase." Commenting on this, Villari says, "If anyone should fail to recognize that this doctrine is purely and exclusively Catholic, and that Savonarola remained steadfastly true to his creed till the close of his life, it would be impossible to find other proofs by which to convince him." The unity of the Church, as the same authority insists, was his most cherished aim. Luther, on the contrary, rent the seamless robe of Christ, and rejected those Sacraments which to Savonarola had always been the divinely appointed channels of grace and strength. Savonarola longed for a reformation, but only in discipline and morals. This is acknowledged by Villari when he says that the prior never attacked the dogmas of the Church, but only those who corrupted them.[4] And another Protestant, the Swiss Sismondi, declares that in seeking to reform the Church, Savonarola never deviated from the pale of orthodoxy. He did not claim the right of examining doctrine, of "private judgement;" rather did he devote all his efforts to the restoration of discipline, to the reformation of the lives of the clergy, and to the winning of priests and laymen to a more perfect observance of the Gospel precepts. "The spirit of Savonarola," wrote Lord Macaulay, "had nothing in common with the spirit, religious or political, of the Protestants of the North."

Quoting Savonarola's utterance on the power of Peter and his successors, his Protestant biographer, Dr. William Clark, says,

---

4   Referring to the Piagnoni after the death of Savonarola, Villari writes: "As we have seen, their religious creed was invariably and strictly Catholic. Even when Rome was besieged by Protestant hosts, and the Florentines were warring against the deadly attacks of the Pope, the Piagnoni refused to coalesce with the followers of the Reformation, and indeed the few Protestants existing in Florence were marks for the popular fury. This was undoubtedly another and most evident sign that Savonarola's doctrines were very different from those of Luther."

When we remember that these are the words of a
man then suffering under a Papal excommunication,
we may easily perceive how far he was removed from
that which we mean by the name of a Protestant.
He was no heretic; he was no schismatic; for he had
plainly declared that the Chair of Peter was the centre of the Catholic Church.

Mr. [Orestes] Brownson, in his Review for April 1852, claimed
that Savonarola had not yet been cleared from error and proved
to have been a good Catholic. This is not only vague but untrue.
We refer to it merely to contrast it with the judgement of intelligent Protestant writers and with the facts. The ex-Calvinist and
freethinker, Bayle, who venomously collected in his dictionary
every opinion inimical to the friar, expresses his surprise at the
Protestant assumption of Savonarola's kinship:

It is very strange that Protestants should number
among their martyrs a friar who during his lifetime
had always celebrated Mass and invoked the saints,
and who at the hour of his death went to Confession
and Communion, made an act of faith in the Real
Presence, and humbly accepted a Plenary Indulgence
granted to him by the Pope.

The Protestant historian von Ranke dismisses the claim of
Savonarola's precursorship of Luther with a few words: "Luther
wished chiefly a reformation of the doctrine, Savonarola a reformation of the morals and the constitution;" and in the same
essay he describes Savonarola as "a reformer who did not fling
off the cowl, but who contended with the Papacy, remaining just
what he was—a friar."

"He was no apostle of reform (as understood by Luther),"
writes John Addington Symonds, in his History of the Renaissance; "it did not occur to him to reconstruct the creed, to dispute the discipline, or to criticise the authority of the Church."
He never went to the length of braving Alexander by burning
his bulls, and by denying the authority of Popes in general. He
desired to purge the Church of sin, but to retain its hierarchy and

its dogmas inviolate. He stoutly maintained the right of the Holy See to temporal dominion, and in this he antagonised the subsequent teaching of Machiavelli and Giucciardini, who wished to strip the Pope of civil power. Mr. Symonds also compares Savonarola to St. Bernardine of Siena and other Catholic reformers and emphasises the fact that none of these ever changed doctrines; they sought only renewal of morals, —a thing, adds this prejudiced writer, that removes Savonarola immeasurably from Hus and Luther.

The well-known Protestant Church historian, Mosheim, ranks Savonarola among the wisest and best men of his age, a pious, eloquent, and learned man, who "having probed the Romish ulcers too freely, suffered for his rashness." Allowing for the peculiarities of gentlemen who say "Romish," we quote this writer who is representative, but he makes no claim to Savonarola as a forerunner of Luther.

Canon Creighton, from whom we have already quoted, readily distinguishes the German Protestant from the Italian Catholic.

> The last days of Savonarola, [says Creighton,] were spent in writing a meditation on the Fifty-first Psalm. This, together with his other devotional writings, enjoyed a wide popularity, and went through many editions. It fell into the hands of Luther, who re-published it in 1523, with a preface in which he claimed Savonarola as one of his own predecessors in setting forth the doctrine of justification by faith only. He writes, in his usual trenchant style, "Though the feet of this holy man are still soiled by theological mud, nevertheless he upheld the doctrine of justification by faith only without works, and therefore he was burned by the Pope. But he lives in blessedness; and Christ canonises him by our means, even though Pope and papists burst with rage." It is not worth-while to examine Luther's grounds for such a statement. Savonarola's words are full of ardent faith in Christ, but Luther's position was far from his mind. He taught nothing which was opposed to the accept-

ed doctrines of the Church, he never denied the Papal headship, and he received submissively the plenary indulgence which Alexander the Sixth granted him before his death.[5]

Rev. W. H. Rule, the title of whose work, *Savonarola and the Dawn of the Reformation*, sufficiently testifies to the author's Protestantism, deplores the fact that Savonarola did not get at the heart of Evangelical Christianity, justification by faith without good works. Indeed, while Mr. Rule is willing to call Savonarola a hero; he refuses to place him among the martyrs, just because he was only "a reformer of morals, and not of doctrines."[6]

Another Protestant writer, to whom we have already referred, Mr. Dinwiddie, though he contends that Savonarola's preaching helped the work of the Saxon friar, still denies that the former had any fellowship with Luther or with any of his forerunners, so-called.[7] We close our references from Protestant authorities with a quotation from Mrs. Oliphant. Speaking of Savonarola's excommunication she says: "This was the moment in which, had he been a Luther, his Protestantism would have developed but such was not the turn of his mind. It did not occur to him to doubt the institutions of his Church, or to question her authority." Of the genuine reformation that was wrought in the sixteenth century by Popes and bishops and saints, Savonarola may be called a forerunner and to his influence in life, his teachings, his example in death, some able Catholic writers have ascribed the salvation of Italy when the flood tide of heresy and iniquity flowed over Northern Europe, and submerged the nations that had accepted the leadership of Luther in revolt against the See

5   Creighton, M., *A History of the Papacy*, Vol III, 246–247.

6   See also the admissions of the anonymous author of *The Life and Times of Savonarola, Illustrating the Progress of the Reformation in Italy during the Fifteenth Century*, London, 1843.

7   *Times before the Reformation*.

of Rome, and in repudiation of the doctrines of the Church of Jesus Christ.[8]

8   For a very satisfactory and exhaustive discussion of this phase of Savonarola's life, we refer the reader to an excellent brochure entitled *Savonarola and the Reformation*, by the Very Reverend Father John Procter, O.P. of Haverstock Hill, London.

V

THE CONTEST WITH THE POPE

✠

THE CONTEST BETWEEN Savonarola and Pope Alexander VI is the crucial point in a life otherwise flawless. In the course of our narrative we related the events as they transpired; we here note the difference between Luther and the Prior of San Marco in their attitude towards the Sovereign Pontiff. At the outset we must put aside all questions as to the personality of the Pope, this being a consideration that is not essential to his authority. Admitting the indictments that have been proved against Alexander, we must bear in mind the words of St. Leo I, "The dignity of Peter does not fail even in an unworthy successor." Nor are we justified in arbitrarily judging motives. Villari is unfair in his frequent charges that Alexander always acted from sinister motives in dealing with Savonarola, nor for these serious accusations does he offer proof. The Pope was obliged to act. He showed considerateness, deference even, for Savonarola. We should abstain, therefore, with greater reason, from imputing to the Pope evil purposes, even if we fail to agree with his policy.

Savonarola defied Alexander, but chiefly in connection with matters political. Bewailing also the abuses of his time, and yielding to the impression that Alexander was not a validly elected Pope, that his acts and commands were neither binding nor effective, Savonarola, holding to the notion, then not uncommon, that a Council was superior to the Pope, subsequently took the stand of an appeal to a Council which he tried to have assembled. In the beginning he was ready to yield obedience, as we have seen; and his language, in addressing the Holy Father, was reverential and submissive. Even when the contest had become acute, the prior maintained a tone of devoted loyalty to the Chair of Peter, of belief in Papal Infallibility. Against the authority of the Church he did not intend to strive, but only against an individual whom he erroneously considered as invalidly holding the Papacy. This judgement, arising from his belief as to Alexander's simoniacal election, involved a decision which it was not for him to make. Here was the grievous error. In his most fiery denunciations against the evils of the day and the abuses in the Church, not one word will be found of disrespect to the teaching power, to the divinely established Papacy. Towards Alexander his language is usually respectful; even when he speaks of wrong-doing, he is not wanting in personal regard for the Pontiff.

Contrast this conduct with the actions and words of Luther towards Leo X. Between them the contest was one entirely theological, the doctrines and sacraments of the Church alone entering into the dispute. Luther was summoned to Rome. What was his answer? "Do you know what I think of Rome? It is a confused collection of fools, idiots, simpletons, blockheads, demoniacs, and devils! Pope and Jackass are synonymous terms!" And then, with the gentleness which marked his later career in speech and writing, he proceeds to tell Pope Leo that he would like to wash his hands "in the blood of the corrupt teachers, cardinals, and Popes, the Roman Sodom contaminating the Church!" Why add to this? It is evident, not only from the German friar's defiance, but from succeeding events and results, that historical truth is shocked and the name of a saintly Catholic is outraged by associating it with the name and teaching of Martin Luther. The Luther monument, erected in Worms in the year 1868, is, therefore, so far as it represents Savonarola, a monumental falsehood. The central figure is that of Luther; other images are those of Melanchthon, Reuchlin, Philip of Hesse, and Frederick of Saxony—all agreeable society. At the base is a smaller group representing Waldo, Wickliffe, Huss, and Savonarola, as the forerunners of the rebel friar of Wittenberg. No calumny uttered during his life would have hurt the Florentine prior so keenly as does this infamous slander, published in an enduring form, four hundred years after his death. "The banner of revolt will be raised against the Church by another, a son of perdition, an instrument of God's terrible judgments," was Savonarola's latest prophecy. The visitation then predicted came with the sack of Rome, when Clement the Seventh was taken prisoner, and when the ruffianly German soldiers robed themselves in the cardinals' attire and proceeded to elect as Pope—Martin Luther! He had raised the standard of rebellion, and Savonarola was his foreteller, but not his forerunner!

VI

SAVONAROLA VENERATED BY
SAINTLY MEN AND WOMEN

✠

A PECULIARLY INTERESTING FEATURE of Savonarola's history is the veneration entertained for him by
saints. Assuredly God guided the chosen souls whose
heroic virtues the Church has crowned by canonization, or by
the minor dignity of beatification, through which they are numbered with those to whom public and solemn honours may be
rendered. That Dominicans should privately revere the memory
of a saintly brother is not surprising.[1] The outspoken homage of

---

1   We must here dissent from Dr. Pastor's charge that the Superiors of the Dominican Order had for a hundred years interdicted the name of Savonarola, thus
antagonising the veneration entertained for him among his brethren. The term
"superiors" is very vague. As to the action of local superiors in such an affair, we
simply state that it carried only the weight of individual opinion, for the matter was
beyond their jurisdiction; as to the supreme heads of the Order, who alone could
outline its policy, history does not bear out the sweeping statement of Pastor. Prudence probably dictated such restrictions as the authorities of the Order imposed
on the veneration of Savonarola's picture and the claims made for his saintliness
during a troubled period, when as yet the name of the martyred prior had not been
vindicated through critical research and historical analysis of the records of his
time. In only two instances, however, did a general of the Order take action against
the veneration of Savonarola. The first occurred four years after his death, when
a command was issued forbidding the brethren of San Marco to call him a saint,
a prophet, or a martyr. Burlamacchi does not hesitate to ascribe this prohibition

acknowledged saints is more significant. Among those who thus regarded Savonarola we may mention the Blessed Catherine of Racconigi, of whom the Breviary states that in heavenly glory she ranks with St. Catherine of Siena, less only in the earthly splendour of canonisation. Blessed Sebastian Maggi; Blessed Osauna of Mantua; Blessed Columba of Rieti; Blessed Mary Bartholomew Bagnesi; St. Catherine of Ricci, and St. Pius V. St. Catharine always kept in her cell a portrait of Savonarola painted by Bartolommeo with the inscription, "A true likeness of Father Jerome, a prophet sent by God."[2] She also possessed, as a sacred relic, one of his fingers, and did not hesitate to ascribe to him the power of miracles. In her life we find the record of various apparitions reported to have been made to her by Savonarola and his two companions in death. The saint declared that he had cured her of a serious illness. Outside of the Dominican Order, St. Francis of Paula, who had prophesied his martyrdom twenty years before it occurred, regarded him as a chosen servant of God. Blessed Juvenal Ancina and Saint John Fisher also held him to be a saint. St. Philip Neri venerated him, kept his image with rays of glory about the head, lovingly called him the Apostle of Florence, and reverently prayed to him.[3] These facts deserve the attention of Catholic writers who are tempted to be more

to the influence of a friar named Sacromoro (whose name we have not previously mentioned), who was regarded as the Judas Iscariot of Savonarola in the hour of his sore need. More than eighty years passed, when, in 1585 the Master General, Father Fabri di Luca, issued another prohibition to all his subjects, forbidding them to mention Savonarola's name; to treat of his life, miracles, companions; to have his image or picture. At that time one of the Medici family, Octavian, was Archbishop of Florence. Father Marchese does not hesitate, on the authority of a letter written by the Grand Duke of Tuscany, which he discovered in the Florentine archives, to indicate this prelate as the occasion of the new edict. St. Catherine de Ricci entered a most respectful but vigorous protest against this prohibition, cautioning the Master General not to take this step. Forty years before, the Tuscan Grand Duke, Cosimo the First, expelled the brethren from San Marco, though he was soon compelled by Pope Paul the Third to restore them. Thus, politics and persecution followed Savonarola after his death.

2   The flames did not entirely consume the body of Savonarola; various relics were secured among the ashes.

3   The publication of an Office in honour of Savonarola by devout admirers we cannot commend. Such a recognition can come, of right, only from the Holy See. We consider claims to sanctity based on such "offices" to be beyond the pale. Proclaiming them as "proof," as indiscreet panegyrists have done, serves no good purpose.

orthodox than the holy men and women that displayed so great
devotion to Savonarola.

VII

Attitude of the Holy See Toward Savonarola

✠

We shall close our sketch with a few words touching the attitude of the Holy See towards Savonarola. Alexander VI acknowledged that he had been misinformed, admitted the virtues of the prior, repudiated all blame for his death, and, according to Burlamacchi, declared his willingness to enrol him among the saints. Julius II, who succeeded Alexander after the brief pontificate of Pius III, knew well the career of Savonarola. That he authorised the painting by Raphael of his likeness with that of St. Thomas Aquinas in the famous fresco, "The Dispute on the Blessed Sacrament," cannot be understood in any but a favourable light. In 1516, Leo X journeyed to Florence, and having gone to San Marco, granted an indulgence of ten years and ten Lents to all who would devoutly visit the prior's cell.[1] In this humble room various relics are still preserved, telling with mute eloquence of the religious life and

1 Pastor insinuates that it was not in honour of Savonarola that Leo X thus favoured this cell. An insinuation is no argument, and it becomes conspicuously worthless, and even suggestive of bias or prejudice, when it ignores facts. Leo X understood his own mind. To what extent he may have thought of reparation to the memory of the great prior, we may not judge; we know, however, that he designated his room as the place of favour; Had it been the Pope's purpose to honour San Marco simply, why did he choose this particular cell? If he wished to signalise

devotion of the illustrious man whose spirit seems still to pervade the place, now no longer the house of prayer, but a "national monument" by the "favour" of Italy's infidel and confiscating government. One hundred years after the death of the Frate, Clement VIII declared that if Ferrara fell into his hands, he would canonise her most illustrious son, —Savonarola. Benedict XIV deemed him worthy of canonisation, and allowed his name to appear in a catalogue published during his pontificate, containing a list of blessed servants of God and of other venerable persons illustrious by their sanctity.[2] And yet he has not been canonised, and probably this honour will never be accorded to him. To us the reason seems simple. That the Holy See should vindicate its dignity by withholding from one who had failed in submission, even under the circumstances of Savonarola's case, the supreme mark on earth of crowned sanctity, ought not to occasion surprise. Moses failed only venially, by a moment's hesitation, a needless stroke, and yet, despite his splendid services, his heroic virtues, this man, meekest among all, went up to Mount Nebo to die, looking out with wistful eyes over the Promised Land, past whose borders he might never go.

It may be, therefore, that Savonarola's name will never be placed on the calendar of the saints. In heavenly glory we believe that he enjoys the beatific vision: for, mindful of the saints who sinned and repented, and applying to him the oft-quoted words of St. Augustine touching St. Cyprian, "If he had faults wherewith to reproach himself regarding his conduct to the Pope, he has fully expiated them by his glorious martyrdom," we may claim that blood and fire washed away whatever stain may have tarnished a career so pure and illustrious.

his esteem for one of the distinguished brethren, why did he not single out the cell of the sainted archbishop, Antoninus, or that of the blessed and angelic painter?

2   Madden states that he had it on high authority that it was one of the earliest designs of Pius IX. was the canonization of Savonarola.

APPENDICES

Savonarola's cell in the Convent of San Marco.

APPENDIX I

*Savonarola's Doctrines, Opinions,
and Sentiments Illustrated
from His Published Works*

F
ATHER QUETIF, O.P., divides the published works of
Savonarola into four classes:

    (a) ascetic;
    (b) prophetic;
    (c) dogmatic;
    (d) controversial and apologetic.

Of the first class there are thirty-eight different publications,
including leaflets, tracts, pamphlets, and regular volumes. Under
nine other headings the numbers thirty sermons on the Sundays
and Festivals; forty-eight sermons on the Prophets Amos and
Zachary; twenty-nine on the Book of Ruth; forty-nine on Eze-
chiel; a volume on Exodus; and one on the Psalms. The second
class includes all the sermons on special texts of the Old and
the New Testaments. The third class contains eight volumes,
and the fourth ten. These writings, covering a great variety of
subjects, offer indisputable evidence of Savonarola's complete

and unwavering Catholic faith. An edition of his works was published during the lifetime of Alexander VI., but this Pontiff expressed no word of condemnation. Under succeeding Popes, Paul III, Julius III, and Paul IV, they were subjected to a rigorous examination, and were declared free from error.[1] During this final examination, St. Philip Neri, who had previously assisted in the publication of a memoir in defence of Savonarola, was constantly engaged in praying that God might crown his venerated patron with Rome's approval. At the very hour, as we read in his life, when the decision was rendered, St. Philip was in the Dominican Church of the Minerva, Rome, most fervently and hopefully praying, and there received the divine assurance of victory. Paul III declared that he would regard as suspected of heresy any man who would charge Savonarola with heresy. "The Triumph of the Cross" became a text-book in seminaries, and St. Philip Neri made it a part of his spiritual direction to urge upon his penitents the reading of Savonarola's books.[2]

We have made a few selections from various parts of his writings, believing that his own words, even though given without special order or connection, and under limitations that involve some obscurity and even some injustice to the writer, will reveal in a manner the character of Savonarola. From his treatise on government, we give no extracts. A clear exposition of the principles underlying government, a vivid picture of the evils of tyranny, this brief but most pithy essay must be read in its entirety, to be judged aright.[3] From other works we would

1   A few sermons—fifteen in number—and the dialogue on prophetic truth were suspended for reasons of prudence, because the circumstances which gave rise to them no longer existed. This prohibition was not a condemnation. It was merely a precautionary measure.

2   Cardinal Barberini, a brother of Pope Urban the Eighth, left by will five hundred ducats to meet the expenses of a new edition of *The Triumph of the Cross*, and of the commentaries on the Fiftieth Psalm.

3   This treatise consists of an Introduction and three parts, each containing three chapters. In the first part he discourses on the following heads: (a) that government is necessary in human affairs—what kind of government is good, what bad; (b) although government by one (a monarchy), when it is good, is of its nature the best, it is not the best for every state; (c) the citizen government (a republic) is the

have been pleased to draw more copiously did our purpose and scope permit.

His meditation on the Fiftieth Psalm, "Have mercy on me, God, according to Thy great mercy," furnishes a passage which has been wrenched from its context, and unjustly offered as a proof that he taught the uselessness of good works, and that salvation comes through faith alone: "Hast thou faith? Well, know then that this is a great grace from God, for faith is His gift; it cannot be obtained by our works, lest anyone should glory in himself." These words simply proclaim the Catholic doctrine that faith, one of the virtues known as theological in distinction from those that are moral, is absolutely the gift of God, the beginning of our supernatural relations with Him, the foundation of our spiritual life. And in this very thought is involved the building of the superstructure of good works, which must be freely done by man, aided by the power of divine grace. Our salvation depends on our willing it. Hence Savonarola, in other parts of his exposition of this Psalm, emphasises the need of good works, springing from a good will. "Who is he that puts bounds to the mercy of God? Hast thou not heard the Lord say that when the sinner repents and turns away from his sins He will no more remember his iniquities? Hast thou fallen? Arise, and mercy shall receive thee. Hast thou been ruined? Cry, and mercy shall come to thee." Assuredly "repenting," "turning from sin," "arising," "crying to the Lord," are evidences of man's will, and work and share in his salvation; and no honest reader of Savonarola's meditation on the Miserere can arrive at any other conclusion than that of his entire Catholicity of teaching. In

---

best for Florence. In the second part he proves (a) that government by one, when it is bad, is the worst, particularly when that one, from a citizen has made himself a tyrant, of whose malice and wickedness he treats in (b), reserving for (c) a consideration of the welfare of a state imperilled by a tyrant, and of the special injury wrought by such a ruler in Florence. In the third part he tells (a) of the institution and manner of government by citizens; (b) what citizens should do in order to perfect a republican government; and (c) of the happiness of those who rule wisely and well, and of the misery of tyrants and their followers.

further testimony, however, we add an extract from his treatise
on humility and prayer:

> The virtues of charity and humility are as the two
> extremes of the spiritual edifice; humility is the
> foundation, charity is the completion of the struc-
> ture. Therefore the faithful should abase themselves
> before God, recognizing that of ourselves we can do
> no good, that without God's help our deeds would be
> evil. It is not sufficient that the mind assent to this
> principle, the soul must feel it profoundly. The will of
> man being free, he must, therefore, use all his endeav-
> ours to crush pride, and become a vessel of grace. For
> this, outward actions will be not only useful, but nec-
> essary. A man of faith must humble himself before
> his superiors and his equals. Let him humble himself
> even before his inferiors. But if on reaching this stage
> he considers that he has accomplished much, then
> outward humility will have increased at the expense
> of his soul; he will lose all merit. Let him, therefore,
> ever be mindful of his own unworthiness.
>
> Let a man pray every day fervently and long. But we
> should always remember that prayer must be accom-
> panied by humility and charity or it will be of no
> avail. As there should be fervour in prayer, and as fer-
> vour may be considered prayer, so in doing deeds of
> charity, it may be said that we pray.

And from one of his sermons on the Psalms we take a passage
that marks his clear teaching of the necessity of grace as the
foundation of all supernatural merit:

> Let all Paradise come here [he exclaims], let the an-
> gels come, let the patriarchs and prophets come, let
> the martyrs come, let the doctors and all the saints
> come, one by one, that I may dispute with them.
> Come, all the elect of God, that I may dispute with
> you. Say the truth, give glory to God, confess the
> truth, if you have the glory, if you are happy and
> blessed by your own merits alone, and by your own
> strength, or by divine goodness. Come here, you es-
> pecially who have been immersed in sins. Tell me, O
> Peter, tell me, O Magdalene, why are you in Paradise?

You certainly sinned like us. Thou, Peter, who didst confess the Son of God, who didst converse with Him, heardest Him preach, sawest His miracles, nay more, who alone with two other disciples sawest Him transfigured on Mount Tabor, and heardest the Father's voice, and nevertheless at the word of a mere woman didst deny Him three times, and yet wast restored to grace and made head of the Church, and now possesses heavenly glory,—whence hast thou obtained such great mercy? Thou wilt say, perhaps, because thou didst return in heart, because thou didst begin to weep bitterly? Yes, O Peter, thanks to the divine goodness which looked upon thee, as the Evangelist says "The Lord turned and looked upon Peter; and Peter went out and wept bitterly." Thou didst not weep until the Lord looked upon thee; thou didst not return in heart until the Lord touched thy heart. Confess, then, Peter, it is not by thy merits, but by the goodness of God, that thou hast obtained such blessings.

In another discourse he asks, "Do you wish Jesus Christ to be your friend? Answer, then, His divine appeal. Your Lord asks you to give Him your heart. Do something for Him then." Assuredly all this is Catholic doctrine. In the *Rule for a Christian Life*, his remembrance to his jailer, he wrote:

Holy living depends on grace; therefore, we must strive to obtain grace, and having secured it, we must endeavour to increase it. To examine our conscience, to meditate on the vanity of earthly things, are means of grace. Confession and Communion move our hearts to receive it. Certainly, it is a free gift of God; but when we have contempt for the world, when a strong desire turns us to spiritual things, then we may feel assured that grace does work. Therefore, perseverance in virtuous living, in good works, in Confession, in Communion, in all that draws to us grace, is the sure way to increase it.

His acknowledgement of the Primacy of the Holy See is complete:

The Church Is one, under one head, in the likeness
and as the image of the Church triumphant in Heav-
en under the reign of Jesus Christ. 'Thou art Peter,
and upon this rock, I will build My Church, and I
will give unto thee the keys of the Kingdom of Heav-
en so that whatsoever thou shalt bind on earth shall
be bound in Heaven, and whatsoever thou shalt loose
on earth shall be loosed in Heaven.' These words
cannot be applied to Peter alone; for as God has
promised that the Church shall continue till the end
of time, they must apply also to Peter's successors.
Therefore, it is manifest that all the faithful should
be united under the Pope, as the supreme head of the
Church of Rome, the mother of all other churches.
Whoever departs from the unity and the doctrines of
the Roman Church, unquestionably such a one departs from Christ.

When he began preaching after his long silence, he made a
public profession of his faith:

I have always believed, and do believe, all that the
Holy Roman Church believes. I have written to Rome
that if I have preached or written anything heretical,
I am content to amend and recant here in public. I
am always prepared to obey the Holy See, and I say
that he who does not obey will be damned. ... I declare and confess that the Church will never fail even
to the Day of Judgment; and that my meaning may be
clear, as there are various opinions as to what is the
Catholic Church, I refer myself to the decision of the
Roman Church established by Jesus Christ.

Enumerating the seven Sacraments (five of which the Reformers in England and Germany rejected), Savonarola taught:

They are instruments, the means established by Jesus
Christ for the working out of our salvation. As these
Sacraments are the channels of grace, and as no one
can be saved without grace, we must receive them as
instruments of the divine help.

On Confession he writes clearly:

> Legal judgement is necessary that proper punish-
> ment may be inflicted for sin; so it is necessary that
> the penitent who submits himself to Christ to be
> healed must await the judgement which Christ
> makes known through His minister. But since a cor-
> rect judgement cannot be pronounced on unknown
> sin, Confession is needed, so that the wound which
> had been concealed is laid bare to the minister of
> Christ in order for a proper healing.

This is from the third book of *The Triumph of the Cross*. In language equally plain he discourses on contrition and satisfaction. From the same volume, the following passage sets forth Savonarola's faith concerning the Holy Sacrifice of the Mass:

> We believe and declare that under the appearance of
> bread, no matter how small, is the Body of Christ,
> whole and entire; and that under the appearance of
> wine, even a drop, is the Blood of Christ, whole and
> entire; and we believe that Jesus Christ, whole and
> entire, is at the same time in Heaven. We say that the
> Body and Blood of Christ are present in the Blessed
> Eucharist, in virtue of the words of consecration, not
> because He comes there from some other place, but
> because the substance of the bread and the wine is
> changed. By the power of the words through which
> Transubstantiation takes place, there are in the Eu-
> charist the Body and Blood of Jesus Christ under the
> appearances of bread and wine, because such is the
> meaning of Transubstantiation. By natural concomi-
> tance the Soul and the Divinity are also present.

Of the Thirty-nine Articles embodying the "faith" of the "reformed" Church of England, the twenty second brands devotion to our Lady as a thing "vainly invented, founded upon no warranty of Scripture, but rather repugnant to the word of God." As an illustration of Savonarola's love for the Queen of Heaven, we here give an English version of the hymn written by him during the plague in Florence, and sung by the people with great fervour and confidence. It is an evidence of Savonarola's poetic talent as well as a proof of his tender devotion to our Lady, a point on which, despite his numerous and loving references throughout his sermons and his commentaries on the Hail Mary, he has been cruelly misrepresented. It is entitled:

MARY, THE STAR OF THE SEA

O Star of Galilee,
Shining o'er this earth's dark sea.
Shed thy glorious light on me,
Maria Stella Maris.

Queen of Clemency and Love,
Be my Advocate above,
And, through Christ, all sin remove,
Maria Stella Maris.

When the Angel called thee blest.
And with transports tilled thy breast,
Twas thy Lord became thy Guest,
Maria Stella Maris.

Earth's purest creature thou,
In the heavens exulting now,
With a halo round thy brow,
Maria Stella Maris.

Beauty beams in every trace
Of the Virgin Mother's face,
Full of glory and of grace
Maria Stella Maris.

A Beacon to the just,
To the sinner Hope and Trust,
Joy of the angel host,
Maria Stella Maris.

Ever glorified, thy throne
Is where thy Blessed Son
Doth reign:
through Him alone,
Maria Stella Maris.

All pestilence shall cease,
And sin and strife decrease,
And the kingdom come of peace,

Maria Stella Maris.

He warns the faithful against unwarranted reading of the Bible, in which counsel he shows his Catholicity as opposed to the radical error of Protestantism:

> He who undertakes to read the Holy Scriptures without being enlightened by a supernatural light,[4] embarrasses and deceives himself. He who thus reads will not understand, he will spend his time in vain. Natural sciences can be acquired through the natural light which reason gives to us; but "the divine science cannot be learned without a special ray of light from God. Hence it happens that many of those who read the Holy Scriptures do not comprehend their beauty, nor do they understand. They fulfil the word of Isaias: The visions of the Prophets shall be unto you as the words of a book closed and sealed, for the blind cannot see colours."

Then he proceeds to show the necessity of purity of heart that the divine light may be of profit:

> Let him, therefore, who would profit by reading the Holy Scriptures, purge himself of sin; let him free himself from worldly cares; let him begin with prayer and in humility; let him withdraw, in the spirit of faith, to the solitude of his chamber. Thus prepared, and fortified by his good works, he will deserve a share in heavenly light whereby he may read unto profit.

In his commentary on the "Our Father," he writes:

> As it is absolutely necessary that grace and our free will should concur, in order that we may obtain the remission of our sins, it is needful, O my soul, if we would deserve God's grace, that we do all in our power, lest in asking pardon for our faults, and persevering in evil, we come to be of the number of those who wilfully tempt God.

---

4   The guidance and assurance in interpretation of the Church.

Had Luther honestly read this passage he would not have quoted Savonarola in defence of his theory of justification without good works. The words of the Dominican are an anticipated protest against Luther's blasphemy: "Sin strongly, but have still stronger faith." How touching is his letter to his father, written when he left his home to become a Dominican:

> The motive which decides me to enter Religion is simply this: the wretchedness and misery of the world; the wickedness of men, their thefts, impurities, and robberies; the pride, idolatry, and blasphemies which so defile our times that we find few who try to load a good life. Hence these lines often come to my mind, and bring tears to my eyes:
>
> Fly from this heartless land,
>
> Fly from this covetous shore.[5]
>
> Indeed, I can no longer endure the appalling wickedness that exists in parts of Italy. Everywhere piety is despised and vice is honoured. What keener sorrow can this life ever bring me? Day after day, therefore, I have implored our Lord Jesus Christ to save me from the abyss; while my heart unceasingly cries out, "Show me, O God, the way in which I should walk, for unto Thee have I lifted up my soul." In His infinite pity God has deigned to show me the way, and I have entered upon it, although it is a grace of which I am entirely unworthy.

How like A Kempis is the letter to some Dominican Sisters who had importuned him for instructions:

> Continual writing is useless, if those who read take no profit by it. Repetition may be useful in sermons, as the spoken word passes and flies, and does not remain impressed on the heart. But written words should be read again and again. The Gospel was not written on paper, nor on stone; it was imprinted on the hearts of the Apostles, and so it wrought miracles.

5   Virgil.

You seek new exhortations, new epistles; but reading much, without profit, you learn nothing. It was more profitable to St. Antony that he learned the words, "Go, sell all that thou dost possess, and give to the poor, and follow Me," than it advantages many theologians to turn over the whole matter of theology. Wherefore, dear Sisters, as there are already enough works in the vernacular for the salvation of the world, we must not needlessly swell the number of tracts and epistles. Rather should we diligently read and meditate on those already composed, endeavouring to put their precepts and counsels into practice.

This lesson to his disciples is one that every true Christian should follow:

Above all things love God with all your heart. Seek His glory more than the salvation of your own souls. Strive earnestly to purify your hearts by frequent Confession and devout Communion that your affections may be raised above earthly things. Never regard yourselves as better than others, even the most sinful. Think ill of no one, well of every one. Often observe silence ; be as much alone as your duties permit. Shun all murmuring, detraction, idle words; let deceitful words and slander be far from your ears, and farther from your tongues. Pray often; meditate (that is, think of God) every hour. Show no haughtiness in word or action. Be not over familiar with those under you; manifest rather a courteous gravity. Being always fearful of sin, and remembering the presence of God, ever ask the grace of perseverance. Renew your good resolutions every day, and thus conforming yourselves with God's grace, in virtue, despair not for any sin.

He concludes by asking prayers that his own life may be conformable to his preaching. The following is a beautiful as well as practical thought:

O women, who glory in your dress, your hair, your hands, I tell you you are not beautiful; you are ugly. If you would behold not hideousness, but true beauty, look at some devout person that is guided by the Holy

Ghost. Observe such a one in prayer, and with the Divine radiance after prayer! You will see the beauty of God reflected on her countenance made like to that of an angel. — He disregards sufferings, and looks forward to a violent death:

Let the Lord's will be done, for the greater our sufferings on earth, the greater will be our crown of glory in Heaven. Let us, therefore, leave all to the Lord he is the Master that useth the tool to His own ends, and when He no longer needs it, He casts it aside, even as he permitted Jeremiah to be stoned to death. Even so will it be with us when we have served His end.

After returning from his interview with King Charles, he spoke to the people thus:

This is a time in which words must give way to deeds, and vain ceremonies to true sentiments. The Lord hath said: "I was hungry, and you gave me no meat; I was naked, and ye clothed me not." He never said: "Ye built not a beautiful church, or a fine convent." He speaks only of works of charity. We must begin our work of renovation, then, with charity.

Of the goodness of God, he says:

Good is of its own nature diffusive, and therefore I, Who am the Supreme Good, diffuse Myself in creation, and I have given being to all creatures, so that every good which is in them is a participation of My goodness. For this I came down among men, was made man, and died upon the cross. This, then, will be the sign by which it will be known who is good. When any one diffuses his goodness among others, and makes them partakers of that good which he has in himself, then he is truly good, and participates in My goodness. Christian life, [he goes on,] does not consist in ceremonies, but in being good, and he who is good cannot refrain from showing his goodness. And in this consists the Christian religion, which is founded in love and charity.

His reference to ceremonies must be taken in the sense in which God Himself condemned of old the ceremonies instituted by Himself when they were no longer animated by faith and love.

> Faith [he said] is omnipotent and despises the life of earth because it is assured of the life of Heaven. The times predicted are drawing near, —the hour of danger, when it will be seen who is truly on the Lord's side. The wicked thought to hinder me from preaching today; but they must know that I have never shrunk from my duty through fear of men. No man on earth, be he great or small, can boast of having hindered me in my office. O Lord, deliver me from these adversaries, who call me a seducer; deliver my soul, for I have no fear for my body. I call as witnesses the Lord, the Blessed Virgin, the angels, and the saints, that the things revealed by me come from God, and that I have received them by divine inspiration in the vigils which I have passed for the good of this people which now plot against me.

He describes the rewards of heaven and the trials of earth:

> But what, O Lord, shall be the reward granted in the other life to him who is victorious in battle? A thing which the eye cannot see, which the ear cannot hear, —eternal blessedness. And what the reward granted in this life? "The servant shall not be greater than his master," answers the Lord. "Thou knowest that after preaching I was crucified; so martyrdom will befall thee also. O Lord, Lord, grant me, I pray Thee, this martyrdom, and make me ready to die for Thee as Thou hast died for me. Already the knife is sharpened for me. But the Lord tells me, 'Wait yet a little while, so that the things may come which have to follow; and then thou wilt use that strength of mind which shall be given thee.'

He warns the righteous of evils soon to come:

> It is the will of God that I should be the first to endure them. I have already told you that I shall meet with great ingratitude, and the lukewarm will treat

me as did the brothers of Joseph, who sold him to the Egyptian merchants. These say that i am no prophet; but they are only bringing about the fulfilment of my predictions. I repeat to you that Italy will be devastated by barbarous nations; and when they shall promise peace and safety, then sudden and repeated destruction shall come upon this perverse Italy.

But you who are righteous make your prayers unto the Lord, and you shall have help. And as for the wicked. Lord, be not angry with them; convert them, forgive them, for they know not what they do. You believe, O sinful men, that you are fighting against the friar, but you only make war on the Lord; because I do not fight against you from hatred of you, but from love of God.

In a sermon against usury and immoderate gains, he says:

Therefore, owing to avarice, neither you nor your children lead a good life. You have already discovered many devices for gaining money, and many modes of exchange which you call just, but are most unjust; and you have likewise corrupted the magistrates in their functions. None can persuade you that it is sinful to lend at usury or to make unjust bargains. On the contrary, you defend yourselves to your soul's damnation; nor does any man take shame to himself for lending at usury, but rather considers those to be fools that refrain from it. And thus, you fulfil the saying of Isaiah: 'They declare their sin as Sodom; they hide it not,' and that of Jeremiah, "Thou hadst a strumpet's forehead; thou refusest to be ashamed." Thou sayest that the good and happy life consists in gain; and Christ says, "Blessed are the poor in spirit, for theirs is the kingdom of Heaven." Thou sayest that the happy life consists in pleasure and voluptuousness; and Christ says, "Blessed are they that mourn, for they shall be comforted," Thou sayest that the happy life consists in glory; and Christ says, "Blessed are you when men shall revile you and persecute you." The way of life hath been shown to you, yet none follow it, none seek it, none learn it. Therefore Christ laments over you. Having endured much to show you the way of life, that all might be saved, He is justly incensed against you and has declared by the mouth of the prophet, "I am weary with calling, my tongue cleaves to the roof of my mouth for all day do I cry with the voice of the Preachers, and no one hearkens unto me."

The following passage shows the tenderness of the Frate's heart:

Behold what love can affect. Take the example of a mother with her child. Who has taught this young woman, who has had no children before, to nurse her babe? Love. See what fatigue she endures by day and by night to rear it, and how the heaviest fatigue seems light to her. What is the cause of this? It is love. See what ways she has, what loving caresses and sweet words, for this little babe of hers ! What has taught her these things ? Love. . . . Take the example of Christ who, moved by the deepest charity, came to us as a little child, in all things like unto the sons of men, and submitting to hunger and thirst, to heat and cold and discomfort. What has urged Him to do this? Love. He spoke now with just men, again with publicans and sinners. He led a life that all men and all women, small and great, rich and poor, may imitate all after their own way, and according to their condition, and thus undoubtedly win their salvation. And what made Him lead so poor and marvellous a life? Undoubtedly charity. . . . Charity bound Him to the pillar, charity led Him to the cross, charity raised Him from the dead, and made Him ascend into Heaven, and thus accomplish all the mysteries of our redemption. This is true and only doctrine, but in these days the preachers teach nothing but empty subtleties.

He deplores the folly of superfluous reading, and the evil works of worldly and sinful priests:

For if thou lackest the spirit of grace, what will it avail thee to carry about the whole book? And, again, still greater is the foolishness of those that load themselves with letters and tracts and writings, so that

they are like unto stalls at a fair. Charity does not
consist in written papers! The true books of Christ
are the Apostles and the Saints; the true reading of
them is to imitate their lives. But in these days men
are made books of the devil. They speak against pride
and ambition, yet are plunged in both up to the eyes;
they preach chastity, and maintain concubines; they
prescribe fasting, and feast sumptuously themselves.

They call me [he says, referring to the installation of
a new Signoria] the son of perdition. Let this be sent
back for answer: The man whom you thus designate
has neither harlots nor concubines, but gives himself up to preaching the faith of Christ. His spiritual children, those who listen to his doctrine, do not
pass their time in the commission of crimes; they go
to Confession, to Communion; they live virtuously.
This friar labours to exalt the Church of Christ, and
you try to destroy it.

Replying to Ludovico the Moor, who had accused him of
teaching disobedience to the Pope, he protests:

It is not true that I have ever declared absolutely that
the Pope ought not to be obeyed, because this would
be very reprehensible, and contrary to those sacred
canons according to which I have always governed
myself. And so, too, it is a false accusation to say that
I have spoken against your lordship. I am affectionate
to all and have no right to speak against anyone in
particular, but if your lordship be turned to God in
that mind which you declare to be yours, then you
have only to persevere; and in this matter you can
have no better judge than your own conscience.

In his defence of his attitude towards the Pope, he said:

Who does not know that the Brief was issued to support my enemies and those of the Republic who disseminated falsehoods and calumnies against me?
Who does not know that my departure would not
only be most dangerous to my own life, but also injurious to this people, and ruinous to its liberty; that
good customs would be abandoned, and religion

come to the ground? It is this indeed that my enemies desire. I therefore believe that the Holy Father
has been deceived by the false accusations of my
detractors; and I obey rather that which I believe to
have been his intention, and will not suppose that he
desires the ruin of a whole people.

We give Savonarola's words. Our comment has already been
made: "Let justice be done though the heavens fall;" and so say
we of obedience to proper authority. The letter of Savonarola
to Alexander VI, in which he gives the reasons why he thought
the Pope's order not binding, we print in full:[6]

> *Most Holy Father* [he writes], I prostrate myself at the
> feet of your Holiness. Why is my Lord angry with his
> servant, or where is the wrong that I have done? If
> the sons of iniquity have spoken falsely of me, why
> does my Lord not inquire of his servant and hear his
> account before believing them? For it is not easy to
> persuade a mind which is already prejudiced.
>
> Many dogs have compassed me, the assembly of the
> wicked have enclosed me, and they say: "Behold! his
> God cannot help him or save him." For your Holiness
> holds the place of God on earth, and they accuse me
> of treason towards you, saying that I do not cease to
> blame you and find fault with you, and so in many
> ways they twist and cruelly pervert the meaning of
> my words.
>
> The same thing was done two years ago, but thou-
> sands who heard me can witness to my innocence, as
> well as my own words, faithfully taken down at the
> time and printed and scattered abroad. Let these be
> brought forward, and read and examined, that it may
> be seen if in them there is anything offensive to your
> Holiness, as these liars so often assert.
>
> Is it likely that I would say one thing and write an-
> other, and so lay myself open to the charge of flagrant
> contradiction? What could be the object or the in-
> tention of such a line of conduct? I only wonder that

6 See Part I., XVII.

your Holiness does not see their wicked madness. As for this great and renowned preacher, he must have little shame or honesty to accuse an innocent man of the very crime of which he is guilty.

His words cannot be hidden away. There are numerous witnesses who have heard him openly attacking your Holiness, and lest I should be accused of falsehood, I could, if necessary, bring forward legal proof. But I have not forgotten that his insolence has already been silenced and condemned, since it is sinful to calumniate anyone, no matter how lowly he may be, much more one who is the Ruler and Pastor of all. Who is so senseless as to be ignorant of this?

For, thanks be to God, I am not so utterly abandoned, so utterly forgetful of my duty, as, without any reason or excuse, to dare to attack and insult the Vicar of Christ, to whom, above everyone else on earth, reverence is due. As for the rest, I have never uttered a word contrary to the Holy Catholic Faith, or contrary to the teaching of the Roman Church, to whose judgement and authority I have ever submitted myself, and ever shall, whenever I am called upon.

And this is what I have always taught, and shall teach with all my strength, at the same time doing my best to rouse men to sorrow for sin and amendment of life by awakening their faith in our Lord Jesus Christ.

The work which I shall shortly bring out on the Triumph of the Cross is a witness to my faith, and from it can be seen if I have ever taught heresy or in any way opposed the Catholic Faith.

Will your Holiness, therefore, turn a deaf ear to these envious and lying tongues, and only believe what has been examined and proved, since many of their falsehoods have already been openly detected. But if all human help fail me, and the wickedness of these impious men gain the day, I will still hope in God and in His help, and make their wickedness so public to the whole world that perhaps at the very last they will repent of their evil designs.

I most humbly commend myself to your Holiness.

From the Convent of San Marco,
Florence, May 22nd, 1497

The character of the sermons he delivered with a view to the reformation of art and artists may be judged from one quotation:

> In what does beauty consist? In colour? No. In form? No. Beauty, so far as composite things are concerned, springs from the harmony of parts and colours; in simple things, beauty is their light. Behold the sim and the stars! Their beauty is in the light they shed. Behold the blessed angels and heavenly spirits! Their beauty is in light. The Divine Beauty, God Himself, is eternal Light. Thus the beauty of man or woman is greater, more perfect, as it approaches the primary beauty. What, then, is this beauty? It is a quality resulting from the harmony and proportion of parts and members of the body. A woman is not beautiful because she has a beautiful nose or beautiful hands, but when all the parts are in correspondence and agreement. The source of this beauty is the soul

Then he proceeds to show the power of virtue and the effects of vice. He lashed the painters of his day who defiled the house of God by representing the Blessed Virgin and the saints after the likenesses of women too well known in the city of Florence, "a great profanation of Divine things with which they filled the churches." We subjoin a few scattered thoughts from his spiritual letters:

> The lukewarm Christian does not have many tribulations in this life, for Satan does not persecute his own. The fervent follower of Christ must encounter great opposition because he is the adversary of the devil. There are three arms, against which Hell's power cannot prevail, which the world cannot overcome, which secure the success of every good work, —strong faith, constant prayer, and humble patience. All cowardice of spirit comes from want of

faith, from ignorance of the goodness of God. The goodness of God is so great that we can surely obtain from Him all we desire for His honour and for our soul's salvation.

Mindful of his experience of men, and as a proof of his devoutly Christian spirit, we close with a quotation from a letter addressed by him to the Brethren of San Marco:

Beware of ingratitude, for it is as a scorching wind that dries up the fount of mercy. I beseech you, that you be mindful of the benefits which you have received from God; especially remember that he has enlightened you, and opened the eyes of your soul, enabling you by the grace of Christ and the renewal of the Holy Spirit to come to perfection. Thus enriched by God, above others, it behoves you, above others, to manifest your gratitude and praise

LIST OF SAVONAROLA'S CHIEF WORKS

The Triumph of the Cross (Four books)
On the Simplicity of Christian Life (Five books)
On Jewish Astrology (Three Books)
Explanation of the Our Father and Hail Mary
Treatise on Humility
Treatise on the Love of Jesus Christ
Treatise on Widowhood
The Lament of the Spouse of Christ
The Soul and the Spirit (Seven Dialogues)
Reason and Sense (Three Dialogues)
Prayer (Two books)
Rules of Prayer and Devout Life
Explanation of the Commandments
The Sacrifice of the Mass and its Mysteries
Frequent Communion

The Sign of the Cross, Advantages and Meaning
Union with God: A Discourse
Letter on taking the Habit of Religion
On the Perfection of the Religious State
Letters to the Brethren of the Order of St. Dominic
Spiritual Reading, For Sisters of the Third Order
Perfection of Spiritual Life
The Seven Rules of a Religious
Meditations on the Psalm, Diligam te, Domine
Meditations on the Various Psalms
The Mystery of the Cross
Manual of Confessors
Sermons for Sundays and Festivals
Forty-Eight Sermons for Lent
Homilies on Holy Writ, etc.

APPENDIX II

SAVONAROLA AND CHRISTIAN ART IN FLORENCE

✠

TO ONE HAVING the slightest knowledge of the history of Florence during the fifteenth century, it must be apparent that the reform initiated by Savonarola would have been incomplete, insignificant, and indeed wholly vain, if the ardent preacher, having combated the pagan education and morals of the time, had spared the paganized art. Florence was another Athens, in which the cult of beauty had assumed a character wholly naturalistic and sensual. True Greeks, by reason of their inconstancy, their levity, their insatiable appetite for novelties; captivated by theories as fanciful as dreams; fond of luxury and of pleasure, —the Florentines were foremost in reviving the antique, and in elaborating an art which, almost wholly excluding the Christian ideal, sought perfection in form alone. Their city, it is true, was speedily filled with magnificent monuments. Even the glory of Rome itself was eclipsed by that of the "City of Flowers." From Germany and beyond, men first sought Florence before visiting the venerable capital of the Roman world.

It was the Medici, and especially Lorenzo the Magnificent, who, above all, directed and encouraged a movement that resulted in a decadence of art, quite as much as in a renaissance: a decadence from the point of view of religion; a renaissance from the materialistic and technical point of view.

During the epoch with which we are concerned, between 1450 and 1491, after the passionate study of the antique marbles; after the discoveries of Uccello; after the wholly profane audacities of Pollajuolo, of Signorelli, and even of Botticelli, to mention no others; after the scandalous adventures of Fra Filippo Lippi, the licence of the painters was restrained by no bounds; and the facts noted by contemporary writers show the absolute, the urgent need of the reform inaugurated by the celebrated prior of San Marco's, a reform based on an ideal more austere and more elevated. The Madonnas were customarily draped after the fashion of courtesans. Vasari relates that a certain father of a family, indignant at the liberties taken by a painter with the very person of the Mother of God, asked him for a Virgin whose religious expression should at least exclude from the mind every impure thought. The painter, Nunziata by name, fulfilled this commission by handing his patron a Madonna wearing a long beard.[1] In Florence, there was more than one artist of renown who boasted of never having had the Faith. The philosophy of Plato was the vogue, along with elegant verses, erotic stories, and indecent pictures. One would hardly believe, were it not affirmed by more than one writer, that mythological subjects were exposed in the very churches, and that the paganism which had corrupted society affected diseased imaginations and debased hearts at the foot of the altar itself.

I mentioned Fra Filippo Lippi. Who does not know that many of his Madonnas are sacrilegious portraits, and that, at the age of fifty, he was not ashamed to carry away from her convent a young novice, whose features he reproduced, time and again, in religious pictures? A crowd of young people, attracted by this novelty, gathered curiously about the compositions of the debauched Carmelite; and it is easy to imagine the impression

1   *Rio: L'art Chretien*, tome 2e; Savonarole.

produced on a society thus depraved by examples emanating from the sanctuary, and therefore not less alluring than dangerous. Some, indeed, of the disciples of Fra Angelico, artists endowed with nobler, purer souls, endeavoured to art. stem the torrent. A Benozzo Gozzoli, a Lorenzo di Credi, a Sandro Botticelli, still did honour to Christian Perugino held the sceptre of religious painting a scepter that would soon break in the feeble hands of this master of the Umbrian school. When Perugino's star declined, it was beneath clouds so dark that they obscured not only his great fame, but even the memory of himself. Botticelli sought to combine mythology with Christianity, fiction with faith, nudities intended to be chaste with devotional compositions intended to excite piety. The task was as difficult, as repulsive, then, as it would be to-day. Against the prevailing tendencies, what could the few heirs of the genius of the primitives effect? However sure their talents, neither means nor influence could they command.

What they could not do, artists as they wore, a man who was neither sculptor nor painter nor architect, but who inspired architects, painters, and sculptors, did effect. This man was gifted with a soul all aflame; with an oratorical talent seldom, if ever, surpassed; genius; with a profound faith and a transcendent and through these gifts and acquirements, swaying men, he was enabled to perform prodigies. Savonarola, it is who did for art in Florence what no other man could do. Studying the celebrated monk of San Marco, what astonishes us is not his possession of certain special gifts, which have indeed been conferred by God on other men in an equal degree; but rather the universality of his gifts, and the variety and breadth of the influence he exercised over his contemporaries.

That he should have been a theologian, a philosopher, an orator, and a writer, may not surprise us; but when we see him engaged with the smallest details of pedagogy, dictating political constitutions, discussing in the ateliers with painters or sculptors questions wholly artistic; when we note that no single subject about which the human mind can be exercised, escaped his clear-sighted vision; and that, through the power of the word, he was a master in all these matters, and that he made his power felt, then indeed we are amazed; and we cannot help regarding Savonarola as one of the most extraordinary men of whom there is a record in the annals of history.

> Savonarola, [says an historian,] might have chosen any career other than that of the cloister; he would have handled the chisel as well as the pen, the brush as well the word; had he wished, he could have been a greater philosopher than Ficino, a more skilful rhetorician than Politician, a poet more admirable than Sannazaro. Heading his sermons, it is evident that he was familiar with all the literary sources known in his day; that he drew inspiration from the Bible, and from Homer, Plato, and Aristotle; that he was acquainted with the doctrine of the so-called Alexandrian school that he had studied astronomy, physics, mechanics, the natural sciences; and that he had especially meditated on the laws of Greece and of ancient Italy.[2]

What a commotion there was in Florence—shall we not say, what a pious revolution—when unworthy magistrates, merciless usurers, lying doctors, instigators of debauchery, and indecent artists were, one and all, reprobated by the sovereign orator whose eloquence flashed like the lightning, and pealed like thunder! Lascivious songs were replaced by chaste canticles, taken out of the old melodic treasures of the church; instead of scenes of violence there were processions of children; and all the arts paid homage to God, the source of every beauty. It should, of course, be remembered that Savonarola belonged to a religious order in which the fine arts had been always cultivated. Hardly had the Friars Preachers been founded when two architects of genius were enrolled among the members, Fra Sisto and Fra Ristoro, both of whom passed almost their whole lives at Florence.[3] They

2   Audin., *Hist, de Leon X.*, vol.I., chap. VIII.

3   The dates are approximately 1225–1285.

completed the palace of the Podesta, reconstructed the Carraja bridge and, as a monument witnessing to the peace established between the Guelphs and the Ghibellines, erected the beautiful church of Santa Maria Novella, which Michaelangelo charmingly called "his bride," and which Richa and Fineschi declare to be, in its style, the most severe, and at the same time the most pleasing, design in all Italy. To these two friars, and not unreasonably, the design of the church of the Minerva, in Rome, is also attributed; there they worked several years, assisting in the construction of the Vatican palace.

Among the pioneers of the order, we find a sculptor too, Fra Guglielmo da Pisa, who devoted a splendid talent to ornamenting the tomb of St. Dominic, at Bologna. In Florence, Giovanni da Campi and Jacopo Talenti were not the only gifted friars who continued the artistic traditions of the order, or who transmitted them to well-trained pupils. The first Dominican miniaturists, and among these the illustrious cardinal, Blessed John Dominici, we trace to Santa Maria Novella and to San Marco. Next comes Fra Angelico, who, like his brother Benedetto, was a miniaturist before being a painter. God has indeed blessed the Dominicans, giving to the order the prince of Christian painting as well as the prince of Theology. And what is beauty but the splendour of truth! Florence, more than any other city in the world, is rich in the treasures left her by the Blessed Angelico. His sublime compositions on the walls of the Convent of St. Mark showed forth to Savonarola the realisation of the ideal as conceived by both these great men. Surely it was not without a providential design that the reformer dwelt in the cloisters sanctified, as well as decorated, by the artist; and that the orator, by the power of his word, gave new life to the peaceful apostolate initiated by the brush of Angelico. And yet it may be that the apostolate of the painter, by its very nature, was more enduring than that of the preacher; for the voice of the orator dies away; we tire of reading his phrases, but we never tire of looking at pictures. As

the Blessed Lorenzo de Ripafracta so well said to Fra Angelico
and Fra Benedetto when the two youths were being trained in
the virtues most becoming their state of life, in the novitiate
at Cortona:

> You have an advantage of which orators are deprived.
> The word cannot reach those who are far off, nor
> does the most eloquent tongue deliver oracles from
> the tomb; but the influence of your heavenly compo-
> sitions will be immortal. During the ages they will
> persist as authentic witnesses, as efficacious preach-
> ers, of religion and of virtue.[4]

Shall we make no mention of Blessed James of Ulm, and of his
school of painting on glass? Or of the renowned Fra Bartolommeo della Porta, a spiritual son of Savonarola, and one of those
most faithful to his memory? Besides these, I might name Fra
Damiano da Bergamo, than whom none has been more cunning in marquetry; Fra Marcillat, distinguished as an architect
and as a painter in oils, and unrivalled as a painter on glass; Fra
Domenico Portigiano, the master founder—but pages would
not suffice, were I to complete the list. In his great work on the
Dominican artists, Father Marchese notes more than forty-five
painters of renown, fifty-five architects, twenty-two painters on
glass, twenty-eight miniaturists, six sculptors, five artists in marquetry, not to speak of all those, who, in Italy, France, Holland,
and elsewhere, have studied and solved the most intricate prob-
lems in mechanics. Though I have confined myself to the arts of
design, I may justly record the name of Jerome of Moravia, who,
more learnedly than anyone else, has written of the ecclesiastical
music of the Middle Ages.[5] Were it my purpose to do justice,
not alone to our masters of long ago, but also to those nearer
to us in time, and whose lives form a part of our own, I could
not forget Father Besson, and the paintings in Santa Sabina, or

4   *Vie du B. Laurent. Année Dominicaine.* Fev. 18.

5   See, in the *Revue Thomiste* for August, 1893, a remarkable article, in which Father
J. Berthier, O.P., prints an eloquent list of the Dominicans who have been leaders
and initiators in the various branches of human learning.

Father Danzas, and the splendid windows of the church of the Dominicans at Lyons.

The aesthetic theories of Savonarola may have appeared extravagant to some, and it is indisputable that considered in themselves, and without a due regard to the circumstances and to the moral deprivation of Florentine society, they may not easily be defended against a charge of exaggeration. He forbade absolutely the study of the nude, or of nature by means of the living model. The antique statues found no favour in his sight. More than one master piece of sculpture, it is said, was forever lost in the so-called "destruction of anathemas,"[6] when cards, dice, and other instruments of gambling were burned, along with harps, guitars, violins; with musical scores of indelicate songs, volumes of improper verse, perfumes, powders, essences, immodest portraits, lascivious paintings, and costly carvings, willingly sacrificed by owners anxious for the salvation of their souls. What was possible at a time when Faith still held sway would certainly be impracticable today; but why judge mercilessly acts that should be measured according to time and place. The public exposure of nudities has always been, and ever will be, dangerous. For a great number, and especially for the young, the study of the nude has proved a snare, in which too many have been caught at the expense of virtue. Savonarola knew whereof he spoke, we may well believe when from the pulpit he declared that if the artists were conscious, as he was, of the ruin done to simple souls by indecent pictures, they would detest their own works.

Recalling the fact that among the people certain statues were designated by the familiar names of the more notorious Florentine beauties, one will readily excuse the severity of the friar in his effort to destroy works which, in the minds of the people, were associated with real objects, only too well known. In an enterprise so arduous, it was, moreover, difficult to trace the exact line at which excess began. Art, forced backward, quickly

6 A name which he gave to profane objects.

retakes its rightful place. Thus, when I see Lorenzo di Credi and Bartolommeo della Porta cast into the flames their studies of the nude, I call their action grand, noble, an act of courage, exemplary, efficacious, educational. To all the admirers of the mere beauty of form, these painters taught the lesson that in art all things are not permissible, and that, to save art from degeneration and from decadence, certain principles of morality must be defended and practised.

The artists of renown who may justly be called disciples of Savonarola are: Sandro Botticelli, Lorenzo di Credi, Perugino, Fra Bartolommeo, and Michaelangelo, who, though a mere youth when Savonarola was active in preaching, ever remained passionately attached to the ideas, and was ever a student of the writings, of the reformer. Notwithstanding the inevitable differences due to temperament and education, each of these great men was, in his own way, spiritually minded and religious. Botticelli we can recognise at a glance by his mannered elegance. His Madonnas are beautiful and full of expression. The Virgin composing the "Magnificat" has always been considered a masterpiece, in which a most artful disposition of the figures is combined with the expression of a sentiment both intense and deep. Lorenzo di Credi was pious and chaste; all he needed was contact with Savonarola, in order that the ideal he had never ceased contemplating should be exalted still higher. Perugino, notwithstanding the decline notable in the work of his later days, did honour to religion with his brush. To have been the father of a whole generation of artists was glory enough; but even this glory was enhanced by the fame of his pupil Raphael, through whom Perugino may be said to have touched the topmost point that the art of painting should attain. Among these men, it was Fra Bartolommeo whose imagination was the more naturalistic. Familiarity with the works of Fra Angelico caused no change in his manner. He draws most like Raphael, and his colouring is that of a Venetian, but occasionally his outlines are hard, and his coloration pleases the eye more than it affects the soul; still he is a great artist, and one of the brightest luminaries of Dominican art.

What can one say of Michaelangelo? His boldness, Savonarola would not, perhaps, have always approved. But how much more chaste he is in treating the nude than were certain Florentines of the fifteenth century who were pleased to call their composi-tions religious. That he exaggerates the cult of the human form, that he counts the muscles too minutely, indeed that he invents muscles in order to enjoy our admiration of the display, —I do not deny; but how puissant he was, how profound, how sublime! And because of these very qualities, is he not related to Savon-arola, the reformer?

For the most part, the disciples of the friar were true to the memory of their master. In the Convent of San Marco, the sacred fire of great art burned ever brightly; and from San Marco, as a centre, radiated the light of the teachings of which Savona-rola was the apostle. Spread far and wide, the writings of the illustrious preacher perpetuated his creative word, which, not-withstanding the tragic events of the year 1498, had not lost its potency. There is not a single historian of the fine arts who fails to mention Savonarola, or to note the influence exercised by him on the artists of his time. This influence writers may esti-mate favourably or unfavourably, but none can deny that it was profound and permanent. Such is the destiny of the orator. The enthusiasm he excites, the tears he causes to flow, the immediate effect produced on the crowd by his word, we know from expe-rience. But to confine within these narrow limits the good that the orator may do to the souls of men; to measure precisely the duration of the effect of his word; to follow the currents that, flowing from his lips, are transmitted down through the ages, —this is impossible. All we need to say is that history echoes and re-echoes the great orators name, and that, to generation after generation, the mere sound of that name recalls the aim and end to which his life was devoted.

FR. BERNARDS MERLIN, O.P.
Rosary Hill, April, 1898

APPENDIX III

A Bibliography

✠

[Editor's note: The following bibliography references many out of print and obscure works, a number of which are of questionable quality, I have elected to present the bibliography as it was originally published in 1898, as many of the works referenced are of critical importance to the student and devotee of Savonarola to the present time. Modern sources and critical editions as well as information on the ongoing Savonarola project have been appended to the end of this same bibliography.]

TO THE READER who may desire to study more closely the history of Florence as it is identified with the career of Savonarola, and the conditions of the times in which he was born, as well as of the age in which he lived, we desire to present a useful bibliography. The *Lives* of Savonarola, by Burlamacchi, and by Pico della Mirandola, are not readily found in public or private libraries. The edition of Della Mirandola's *Life* which we have used, is the one printed in Paris in 1674. Besides the *Life* this edition contains the same author's, *Apology for Savonarola, as against his unjust excommunication.* This *Apology* was published as a separate volume as early as 1521, at Wittenberg; and this earlier edition we have controlled, as well as the later. The *Life* by Burlamacchi may be found in the *Miscellanea* of Stephen Baluzius (edited by Mansi), published at Lucca, in 1701. Besides the *Life*, this volume also contains valuable letters of Savonarola, of Alexander VI, and of contemporary princes; as well as Father Paul Bernardine's defence of Savonarola under excommunication.

The *Cedrus Libani*, by Father Benedict, is printed in the Archivio Storico Italiano. His *Vulnera Dillgentis*, so-called from the text he used, "Better are the wounds of a friend than the kisses of an enemy," is rare. In the *Vulnera Diligentis*, Benedict, after his return from exile (a punishment inflicted on him for his armed defence of Savonarola on the night when San Marco was stormed), began by voice and pen to prove the forgeries of the iniquitous Ceccone, the notary who corrupted Savonarola's statements. Benedict resorted to sarcasm as well as to criticism, mercilessly lampooning the friar's enemies. He excited such opposition that he was finally imprisoned and tortured. While confined to a cell, his undaunted spirit devoted the lingering hours to the writing of the *Vulnera Diligentis*, an animated and loyal defence of his master. Noting works within the reach of all students, we mention first the writings of the Frate's contemporaries:

1. *The Memoirs of Philip de Commines*
De Commines was the French ambassador to Florence in the time of Savonarola and was personally acquainted with the stirring events of that period.

2. *History of the City of Florence*, by Nardi, an eyewitness of the execution of Savonarola.

3. *History of Florence*, by Machiavelli, a work of less value than the preceding, apart from the character of the author and his dangerous principles.

4. *History of Italy*, by Guiccardini, of whom Montaigne says in his "Essay of Books," that "of so severall and divers armes, successes and effects he judgeth of; of so many and variable motives, alterations and counsels that he relateth, he never referreth anyone unto vertue, religion, or conscience, as if they were all extinguished and banished the world; and of all actions how glorious soever in appearance they be of themselves, he doth ever impute the cause of them to some vicious and blame-worthie occasion, or to some commodities and profit." At greater length Montaigne exhibits the Florentine's methods of writing history, but this warning word is sufficient. Following these, we place, in due order:

5. The third volume of the Dominican Father Touron's *Histoires des Hommes Illustres de l'Ordre de S. Dominique*.

6. The continuation of the *Annales Ecclesiasticae* of Cardinal Baronius, by F. Abraham Bzovius, O.P.

7. *Scriptores Ordinis Praedicatorum*, by Father Quetif, O.P., continued by Father Echard, O.P.

8. The Dominican Father Marchese's writings.

a. *San Marco, Illustrato e Inciso*,

b. Appendices 23 and 25 in the *Archivio Storico Italiano* (very valuable for the insight they give into Savonarola's private life).

c. *Lives of the Most Eminent Painters, Sculptors, and Architects of the Order of St. Dominic*,

whose title is given in English, the Rev. C. P. Meehan translated this work, and published it in Dublin, in 1852. Father Marchese worked diligently and well in bringing to light many previously unknown letters and documents, and has written conscientiously and learnedly in defence of Savonarola.

9. *Jérôme Savonarole, sa vie, ses prédications, ses écrits*, par F. T. Peruens, published in France in 1853, but not as yet translated into English.

10. *Histoire de Florence depuis la domination des Médicis jusqu'à la chute de la République*. 3 vols. Paris, 1888–1890, par F. T. Perrens.

M. Perrens, as we have stated in the body of this book, received generous assistance from the Dominican Father Marchese. The studies of M. Perrens are good. His conclusions, however, do not always agree with our own.

11. *The Life and Martyrdom of Girolamo Savonarola, Illustrative of the History of Church and State Connection*, by R. R. Madden.

This work, published in London in 1853, is of considerable value. It is full, exhaustive, and perhaps needlessly detailed. The author's purpose was to offer proof of the evils arising from a connection between Church and state. His historical references and reflections are copious. He is an ardent admirer of Savonarola but professes to view the held impartially. To the teachings and prophecies of the friar he devotes several chapters, giving generous extracts from his writings, notably a translation of the treatises on the rule of Florence, on prayer, and on the Our Father; and also a spirited version in English of several of Savonarola's hymns, together with the original text in Latin or Italian; and, in an appendix, a list of all his works. A second appendix containing an enumeration of biographies and histories consulted by Mr. Madden will be found helpful. To this author, we are indebted for the metrical translation of the hymn in honour of our Lady published in the second part of our sketch. Despite some inaccuracies indicating hasty writing, but not of sufficient importance to detract from the substantial value of his work, and despite the fact that he wrote as an opponent of the temporal power of the Pope, and with a set purpose of supporting a theory (a disposition which urges a man to subordinate even his hero to his purpose), these volumes by Mr. Madden will be found of interest.

12. *Gli Eretici d'Italia*, by Cesare Cantu.

13. *Storia d'Italia*, by Cesare Cantu.

14. *Storia Universale*, by Cesare Cantu.

These learned works, by one of the greatest among modern historians, need no commendation here.

15. Milman's *Essays on Savonarola, Erasmus, etc.*

16. *View of the State of Europe during the Middle Ages*, by Henry Hallam; and his

17. *Introduction to the Literature of Europe in the Fifteenth, Sixteenth, and Seventeenth Centuries.*

Two works of great research and broad scholarship, notwithstanding the author's prejudices, and his omission, in the latter, of all mention of Savonarola.

18. Michelet's *Renaissance*, a part of his History of France.

Michelet's bitter prejudices are so well known that we are not inclined to esteem highly his estimate of any person, be it favourable or unfavourable.

19. *Üeber die Kunst der Dominicaner in 14 und 15 Jahrhundert*, by Hettner, and his

20. *Renaissance und die Dominicanerkunst.*

21. *Renaissance in Italy*, by John Addington Symonds, a work in live parts that practically form a complete scheme of treatment.

In *The Age of the Despots*, considerable space is given to Savonarola. As Mr. Symonds is a gentleman who uses the word Romish, and rolls under his tongue, as a choice morsel, "Jesuitical hypocrisy," we believe that further criticism is unnecessary.

22. *The Italian Republics*, by Sismondi, and his

23. *History of the Revival of Liberty in Italy; of its Progress, its Decline, and its Fall.*

Sismondi was a Swiss Protestant, an inheritor of Genevan traditions, and therefore a man who will bear watching when he touches matters concerning the Papacy. We quote Sismondi and Symonds chiefly because of their testimony to the Catholicity of Savonarola.

24. *The Life of Lorenzo de Medici, called the Magnificent*, by William Roscoe, and his

25. *Life of Leo the Tenth.*

Mr. Roscoe's works, which were once highly esteemed because of the rarity of English books dealing with the Italian Renaissance, have little value so far as the personal history of Savonarola is concerned. According to the distinguished

Englishman, the great Italian was a dangerous fanatic who met a deserved fate.

26. *Du Vandalisme et du Catholicisme dans l'Art*, par M. Rio, a part of which, *La Poésie Chretienne dans l'Art*, contains a beautiful tribute to Savonarola.

27. *Life of Michelangelo Buonarotti*, by J. S. Harford.

Of Mr. Harford's interesting work, we have already spoken in a note.

28. *Storia della Letteratura Italiana*, by Tiraboschi, who was a Medicean.

29. *Storia della Letteratura Italiana*, by Cantu.

30. *Christian Schools and Scholars*, by Rev. Mother Raphael Drane, O.P.

This work holds a high place in its line; indeed, it may be considered a classic.

31. *Lives of the Most Celebrated Painters, Sculptors, and Architects*, by Vasari.

As a Medicean, this author's judgement is partisan.

32. *The Life of St. Philip Neri*, by Cardinal Capecelatro.

33. *The Life of St. Catherine de Ricci*, by Pere Bayonne, O.P., translated into English by the Dominican Sisters, Albany, N.Y.

34. *The Life of St. Antoninus, Archbishop of Florence*, by F. Touron, O.P.

35. *The Life of Blessed Giovanni of Fiesole, better known as Fra Angelico*, by the same.

36. *History of the Popes*, by Dr. Ludwig Pastor.

This is the latest and best work that has appeared on the Papacy. It supersedes all others, and renders needless any special reference to the work of Christophe *History of the Papacy in the Fifteenth Century*, or to von Ranke's *History of the Popes*.

37. Von Ranke's Savonarola *und die Florentinische Republik gegen Ende des fünfzehnten Jahrhunderts*, an essay published in 1887, as a part of a volume entitled *Historisch Biographische Studien*.

Of this suggestive study we have already spoken. Following it is a *Criticism of the accounts of Savonarola by Pico (della Mirandola) and by Burlamacchi.* Von Ranke argues that the work attributed to Burlamacchi, and written in Italian, is not his; though it may be an edition of a manuscript of his, to which another writer made additions, using freely the Latin life written by Pico. Von Ranke's critique is supported by quotations from the text of Pico as well as from that attributed to Burlamacchi. The facts are, no doubt, as he states them, but von Ranke's conclusions do not affect the credibility of either one of the time-honoured authorities. Though Pico and Burlamacchi frequently agree verbally, yet the two writers are nonetheless distinct and original sources. To explain their agreement may not be easy, but it is their differences that establish their independence and their reliability.

38. *Savonarole et la Statue de Luther à Worms*, par le Père Rouard de Card, O.P.

39. *The Life and Times of Jerome Savonarola*, from the Italian of Pasquale Villari, the latest edition having been published at New York in 1890.

Professor Villari is not a Catholic. He writes as an advocate for his hero and sees little good or honesty in Alexander VI, whom he does not treat with fairness. The political side of the great prior's character he contemplates with special satisfaction. Nevertheless, he views with more sympathy than does Pastor the mystical and the prophetic spirit in Savonarola, and renders a more competent judgement than that of the distinguished German in discussing the merits of Father Bayonne's *Study*. For historical facts, Villari may be safely followed, despite the colouring of his opinions. In the preface to his work, he refers freely to what might be called the Savonarola literature, especially of the nineteenth century.

40. *Étude sur Jérôme Savonarole après des nouveaux Documents*, par le Rp. Bayonne, O.P.

Father Bayonne died before he could realise his entire plan. He earnestly laboured to prove the prophetic power and saintliness of Savonarola, but his work was withdrawn from circulation for reasons of prudence, and not because of any official censure.

We refer to Bayonne's work because it is so frequently mentioned in biographies and histories of Savonarola; we also desire to characterise it as required by the law of the Dominican Order.

41. *Il vero Savonarola e il Savonarola di L. Pastor*, Paolo Luotto, published in Florence, 1897, by Le Monnier.

Like Pere Bayonne, Professor Luotto died before he could see the crown of his labours on behalf of Savonarola. His important work in the volume named is the latest addition to Savonarola literature if we except the centennial review mentioned in this Appendix. Professor Luotto defends Savonarola against the charges brought by Pastor, who, in a subsequent pamphlet, replies to the Italian writer, though he advances no new argument, merely re-affirming the statements made in his *History of the Popes*. The unfriendly article that appeared in the *Civilta Cattolica* (March 5, 1898), reviewing both of these publications, has occasioned much indignation among the admirers of Savonarola, who cannot understand the motive inspiring the severe treatment accorded to the Dominican.

Pastor's Pamphlet was published in Freiburg, by Herder, and is entitled *Zur Beurtheilung Savonarolas Kritische Streifzüge*.

42. *Savonarola and the Reformation*, by Rev. J. Procter, O.P.

This is not the last word of Rev. Father Procter in defence of the much-maligned Frate.

43. *Savonarola. His Life and Times*, by William Clark.

Though the volume is pleasantly written, the author is inimical to the Papacy.

44. *Studies in Church History*, by Rev. Reuben Parsons.

The third volume deals with Huss, the Councils of Basel and Constance, the conspiracy of the Pazzi, Alexander VI, Savonarola, etc.

45. *The Makers of Florence*, by Mrs. Oliphant.

This work treats of Florence in a very interesting manner. To Savonarola, a good portion of the volume is dedicated, while the chapter on the Piagnoni painters may be considered a supplement to his life. Mrs. Oliphant is a champion whose spirit may be judged from one sentence:

And Florence, to which such springs of new life and freedom had come, inspired by that Dominican whom she slaughtered in her public square, fell into a decay of all her noble qualities, which was not beautiful.

46. *Romola*, a romance by George Eliot.

The noted Englishwoman gives a vivid picture of Florence in the last decade of the fifteenth century, and a fairly accurate portrait of the great preacher.

47. *Savonarola, a Tragedy*, by the Poet Laureate of England, Alfred Austin.

48. *History of Philosophy*, by Cardinal Gonzalez, O.P.

Though written in Spanish, and as yet only translated into French, we give the English title of this very valuable work of Cardinal Gonzalez as a translation of it, which will, we hope, soon be published.

49. *Apology for Christianity*, by Rev. Albert M. Weiss, O.P. This very able work has already been rendered into French from the original German. Father Weiss is justly regarded as among the foremost sociologists of the world. He treats, in an admirable manner, the Renaissance. In this list, we have not set down the works of Napier, Dinwiddle, and others named in our earlier pages. We have enumerated only volumes easily obtained. Villari and Madden mention others, available chiefly to the scholar or to the searcher in great libraries.

A review entitled: *Quarto Centenario della Morte di Fra Girolamo Savonarola* (Fourth Centenary of the Death of Friar Jerome Savonarola) is in the course of publication at Florence. Besides letters addressed to the committee in charge of the celebration, by the present Master-General of the Dominican Order, the Most Reverend Father Fruhwirth; by Cardinal Bausa, O.P., Archbishop of Florence; and by other cardinals, bishops, and eminent persons, ecclesiastic and lay, an interesting account will also be found, in this review, of the entire celebration commemorating the fourth centenary of Savonarola's death.

MODERN WORKS
These works are diverse in nature but are included to give the reader as many resources as one can currently find in English.

Works by Savonarola:
1. *Prison Meditations on Psalms 51 and 31* (Reformation Texts with translation: Biblical Studies, Vol. 1) (English and Latin Edition), translated by John P Donelly S.J. (Marquette University Press)
2. *Apologetic Writings* (The I Tatti Renaissance Library), edited by M. Michele Mulcahey, (2015, Harvard University Press)
3. *Selected writings of Girolamo Savonarola*, translated and edited by A. Borelli & M. P. Passaro, (2006, Yale University Press)
4. *A Guide to Righteous Living and Other Works*, ed. Konrad Eisenbichler (2003, Toronto, Centre for Reformation and Renaissance Studies)
5. *The Compendium of Revelations*, ed. Bernard McGinn *Apocalyptic Spirituality: Treatises and Letters of Lactantius, Adso of Montier-en-Der, Joachim of Fiore, the Franciscan Spirituals, Savonarola* (1979, SBCK Publishing)

Biographies & scholarly works:
1. Weinstein, Donald, *Savonarola and Florence: Prophecy and Patriotism in the Renaissance*; (1970, Princeton University Press)
2. Weinstein, Donald, *Savonarola: The Rise and Fall of a Renaissance Prophet*; (2011, Yale University Press)
3. Martines, Lauro, *Fire in the City: Savonarola and the Struggle for the Soul of Renaissance Florence*; (2006, Oxford University Press)
4. Schnitzer, Joseph, *Savonarola*, vols 1 & 2, 1924
    [Editor's note: these two volumes have never been translated into English from German and are out of print except in scanned editions.]

5. Olin, John. C, *The Catholic Reformation: Savonarola to St. Ignatius Loyola*; (1994, Fordham University Press)

6. Strathen, Paul, *Death in Florence: the Medici, Savonarola and the Battle for the Soul of the Renaissance City*; (2015, Pegasus Books)

7. Ridolfi, Roberto, *The Life of Girolamo Savonarola*, translated by Cecil Grayson, (1959, Alfred A. Knopf)

[Editor's note: sadly, this brilliant work is out of print, it is however available online via the internet archive.]